I072089

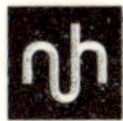

Notting Hill Editions is an independent British publisher. The company was founded by Tom Kremer (1930–2017), champion of innovation and the man responsible for popularising the Rubik's Cube.

After a successful business career in toy invention Tom decided, at the age of eighty, to fulfil his passion for literature. In a fast-moving digital world Tom's aim was to revive the art of the essay, and to create exceptionally beautiful books that would be cherished.

Hailed as 'the shape of things to come', the family-run press brings to print the most surprising thinkers of past and present. In an era of information-overload, these collectible pocket-size books distil ideas that linger in the mind.

Michael Collins is a contemporary art photographer and writer. The recipient of numerous Arts Council England grants, his work is in many British and overseas collections including the V&A, the British Library, and other private collections. He has been picture editor of the *Telegraph* magazine, the photography critic for the *Daily Telegraph* and has written for many publications, including the *Guardian*, the *Financial Times*, the *Independent* and *Granta*. His most recent book of photography is *The Nuclear Sublime*.

Will Self is a writer; he lives in London.

BLIND CORNERS

Michael Collins

–

Introduced by

Will Self

Notting Hill Editions

Published in 2025
by Notting Hill Editions Ltd
Mirefoot, Burneside, Kendal LA8 9AB

Series design by FLOK Design, Berlin, Germany
Cover design by Tom Etherington
Creative advisor: Dennis PAPHITIS

Typeset by CB Editions, London
Printed and bound by Imak Ofset, Istanbul, Turkey

Copyright © 2025 Michael Collins
Introduction copyright © 2025 Will Self

The right of Michael Collins to be identified as the author of this work
has been asserted by him in accordance with section 77 of the Copyright,
Designs & Patents Act 1998. All rights reserved.

The right of Will Self to be identified as the author of the introduction to
this work has been asserted by him in accordance with Section 77 of the
Copyright, Designs & Patents Act 1998. All rights reserved.

Every effort has been made to trace copyright holders and to obtain their
permission for the use of copyright material in this book. The publisher
apologises for any errors or omissions and would be grateful if notified of
any corrections that should be incorporated in future reprints or editions
of this book.

This book is sold subject to the condition that it shall not, by way of trade
or otherwise, be lent, resold, hired out or otherwise circulated without
the publisher's prior consent in any form of binding or cover other than
that in which it is published and without a similar condition including
this condition being imposed on the subsequent purchaser.

A CIP record for this book is available from the British Library

ISBN 978-1-912559-65-7

nottinghilleditions.com

To Rosa

Contents

WILL SELF

– Introduction –

When did it begin, this intense revulsion I feel from the specular culture of our era? I asked myself this question again .... and again, at almost every page of this haunting, paradoxically elegiac collection of essays on photography. (Paradoxical, because one thing's for certain, while photography is itself always a sort of posthumous shock: the epitaph of a moment – it isn't going away any time soon.) While I've felt nothing but disgust for photography of all kinds for over a decade now, nevertheless, Michael Collins – for as long as I keep reading him, and for a considerable while after – persuades me not only of its significance as an art-form, but also of the beauty of individual photographs: indeed, that they partake of the auratic not despite the age of art's technological reproducibility, but precisely because of it.

A decade ago, I remember beginning to have to fight with selfie-stick-wielding tourists in order to cross Westminster Bridge when walking home from the West End; it was a time when the ownership and use of mobile phones and their cameras had moved from the ebullition of universality, to some sort of boiling point: no hand was complete without a lens, while those hands, hydra-like, continually bifurcated, sprouting new appendages, each with its own lens. I remember reading around that time that 'peak photo' had been reached, understood as that year in human history when more photographs were taken than the sum of all those taken in all preceding years. I also visited the Large Hadron Collider at CERN outside Geneva that year, and circumambulated the fifty-kilometre particle accelerator, partly above ground, and partly below – a progress that juxtaposed the scenic Jura escarpment with Alician descents into forty-storey holes, at the bottom of which I found four-storey-high digital cameras being laboriously prepared to capture – in inconceivably infinitesimal fragments of time – images of the unimaginably events this very large installation was built to enact.

For Collins – a landscape and architectural photographer, principally, whose own highly accomplished work is made using equipment that demands long exposure times – the parallax view is understandably also temporal as much as spatial; and it's another of the great benisons of this collection that it draws disparate events in the history of the specular culture into tighter proximity as the elegant line of Collins's prose pans past.

If peak photo was around 2015, then peak art occurred sometime in the mid-1970s. (At least, this was what was vouchsafed to me by Nicholas Penny, the art historian and onetime director of the National

Gallery.) This being understood as the year in which the total value of contemporary artworks sold at market, exceeded that of all artworks of all previous eras. Yes – I know. Staggering. Enough to shake the lens and blur one's image of reality, such that the human figures – the commoditising Hirsts and Koons and Emins – appear as so many wormy blurs traversing the pictorial space.

Vitally concerned by the way in which the physical properties of photographs are obnubilated by their ubiquity, as an essayist Collins is a kind of modern Eadweard Muybridge; but whereas the pioneering photographer studied motion in nature (and its troubling subset, *soi-disant* 'humanity'), these writings are a series of limpid prose-portraits of the technological development of photography and its impact on the collective psyche. The collection comprises notes towards a historiography of photography – placing the practice, schematically, within the overall use and improvement of reprographics – together with tentative excavations of a very personal kind of inner space.

Collins is, one feels towards the end of this collection, always the still and silent man, poised beside his own view camera – a tripod-mounted mechanism (a head-on-legs), that demands of its user a period of studied concentration, looking not through the lens but standing alongside it, as if that lens were also in some sense creaturely. There Collins is, out on the bleak Hoo Peninsula, between the Thames and the

Medway estuaries – or, as I prefer to think of it, the elemental Isle of Grain – waiting for the opportune moment to push the button, open the shutter, and let the full light of reality flood in.

Joseph Conrad's Marlow told his tale of the heart of darkness aboard a yacht moored off the Isle of Grain. Collins has one to tell as well: he describes the way he and his lens interrogate the muddy foreshore of this strange faraway nearby – an expansive fretwork of creeks and muddy islets – in the process, retrieving the buried history of its curious appearance: like the virtual consuming the actual, for decades men laboured digging up the clayey mud to be made into bricks. Bricks that built the city Marlow pronounced to be also 'one of the dark places of the earth'.

It's out of this civilised darkness – in the story, a visible nimbus of coal smoke hanging over the metropolis to the west – that photography flashes; and while Collins doesn't dwell on it, the medium's claim to produce artworks rather than mere artefacts, surely rests in part on the perishability of film stock, and the breakability of the old glass negatives. Those of us who belong to Collins's generation thought the ubiquity of the photograph would never end – the snapshots seemed to sift through the long and dull afternoons as dust does in sunbeams – but of course it did. While cash is no longer king.

With each succeeding year there are fewer and fewer physical photographs extant from the pre-digital era. It's an unavoidable accretion, therefore, of the auratic – as it were a verdigris on the object, like the gabardine veils that seem to swag across the coastal freighter, run aground off the coast of the Isle of Wight in a forever fifties, sepia and yet more sepia still. The decent draperies of a past that Collins twitches gently apart with the tender melancholy of a bashful voyeur; for if it's the case that every reprographic technology creates its own suspension in its viewers' disbelief, each more faithful than the last, so it is that to understand what's happened requires a deeper sort of fidelity to the past: a willingness to take it on its own provisional terms, rather than subjecting it to the absolutism of the present.

Andrei Tarkovsky entitled his lyrical examination of his own *métier* 'Sculpting in Time', and while Collins is working in a parallel medium, there remains a point – long before infinity – where their projects intersect. Both photographer and cinematographer view the exposure of a light-sensitive surface as fundamental to the production of images – rather than any fine-motor control, or otherwise felt, haptic praxis. Just as the optic nerve itself – like some thick hank of gooey cabling – is plugged more or less directly into the brain, so abandoning figuration by hand brings conception and execution into tight proximity. Herein lies the absolute intimacy of photography – its capacity to abide with us. Muybridge said that each discrete image itself contained a lifetime – and it feels that way, doesn't it, when you unearth the old scallop-edged black-and-white snapshot from the prolapsed old cardboard trunk at the back of the once aged – now dead – relative's garage.

Collins duets with this dangerous *douceur de la vie*; a honeyed mood that forever teeters on the edge of outright nostalgia – yet doesn't succumb. His discursive writing about the group shot of the residents of Tenby in South Wales, on Coronation Day, 1952, like his analysis of the poetics of mid-century family snapshot portraiture (Velázquez goes all Kodachrome in a welter of colloidal chemicals and pigments), is an attempt to redeem all those apotheosised moments. It was Susan Sontag who memorably – *pace* Nietzsche – annulled the style/content distinction in fictive prose – and it's a different mode of this dichotomy she also identifies in photography's elision of the objective process with the subjective act: what the lens frames will be recorded, in its entirety, right down to details that, when enhanced, become unknowable and otherworldly: data about the human condition of a finer grain and a denser weave than we can possibly feel, as if it were the nap of some long-gone Burton suit jacket, hung in a dusty wardrobe of the mind, with our numb fingers alone.

In pushing his own medium to the limit of its capacity to resolve the photograph into pure data, Collins also duets with Sontag: for he acknowledges at the same time the absolute errancy that may be consequent even upon this innocent act: choosing the precise moment to open the shutter and let the right light in. He quotes the Russian saying: 'As inaccurate as an eyewitness' – and it's difficult not to be overwhelmed, when we consider the history of reprographic technology as the mechanisation of lying (considered as one of the fine arts): Collins reminds us that the first camera lucidas and obscuras were used by artists such as Caravaggio who wanted to effect levels of realism not obtainable by the naked eye. His colleagues are Hooke with his *Micrographia*; and Descartes, that *res cogitans* with no belief in *res extensa*.

McLuhan observes that when one medium of superior efficiency – print as against manuscript copying, photography as against drawing – supplants another, for some time afterwards the two continue together, in tandem; and indeed some – monks, hipsters – may be convinced for a considerable period that nothing much has changed. But the inception of the specular technologies in the nineteenth century is of a different order – consider the wagon-wheel effect, easily witnessed using a zoetrope or magic lantern, the precursor technology to the panoramas and dioramas Collins hymns as not inchoate forms of the film camera assemblage, but nascent art forms with their own associated psychology – individual and collective – and their own emergent cultures, soon to be superseded. Which is how the world's slide carousel turns.

The uncanny stillness and even reversal of spoked

wheels (or, indeed, the blades of fans, or plane propellers), when stared at, establishes that human vision is, indeed – as Flann O'Brien's speculative philosopher in *The Third Policeman*, De Selby, believes – composed of a series of still images that the mind flicks through, as if it were a flicker book, to create the illusion of motion. What further hypothesis – rather than mere voyeurism, *à la* Isherwood – is required to elide the human subject (whose consciousness can also be said to be comprised by the inconceivably rapid succession of myriad still images), with the camera? Indeed, as the camera – 'room' in Italian – is to the subjective consciousness, so is what McLuhan termed the 'Gutenberg mind', to that bound and serially interleaved phenomenon, born of the associated medium: the book.

Collins, a former picture editor on a national British newspaper, will well appreciate the way an image can be worth thousands more monetarily than any mere words; he'll recall, as well, an advertisement for the *Guardian* newspaper from the 1980s that saw those paragons of the fourth estate professing themselves free from any such intent, by reason of their own deployment of the following sequence. The first photo shows a uniformed white policeman in hot pursuit of a Black man. In the believing-itself-yet-to-wash-whiter Britain of Thatcher's willing executioners, such a cut forced this card: the Black man is perp', to the prospective *Guardian* reader. But lo! The second shot is cropped differently – revealing that the viewer's interpretation of the first has, indeed, been prejudicial eisegesis: here, with a wider view, we see that both Black man and white man are in pursuit of a third man – white, of course – who is the true perp'.

How is the Black man revealed to be a plain-clothes policeman rather than a malefactor? (Not that the two are by any means mutually exclusive.) Well, the *Guardian*-reader-in-waiting now sees that he's straight-edge: neat hair, jacket, etcetera; even as they appreciate – given the proclivities self-selected for by the advertisement's subliminal message – that it's their superior intellect and moral probity that's enabled them to go there.

Collins avers that photography is all about content – but with this example we can see how that content encodes symbols quite as much as it faithfully reproduces images. Which is why its veridical status must be challenged again and again: if the argument is that photography relieved draughtsmanship and colouring of the burden of portrayal, then Collins resiles: for him, it's an art form quite as able to interrogate ways of seeing as it is of merely gaping. To set a camera up in the chimpanzee enclosure at London Zoo, and have the apes photograph the humans goggling at them – as Collins did – is as much to question the notion of consciousness and its associated personhood, as it is to try and determine whether the important thing about a photograph is whether the person who took it was fully conscious of the effect they managed to produce.

True of Niépce when he aimed his lens over the balustrade outside his dormer window. Collins wants photography to be no longer grudgingly admitted as an art form, on the grounds that its reproducibility is inbuilt – but considering the way art itself continues on its Cartesian route, collapsing all *res extensa* into *res cogitans*, as the West reaches a sort of Zeno-point of conceptual aridity, perhaps a better argument is that photography deserves to be considered the artwork of the age precisely because of this: the cybernetics of wet and hardware required for it to work.

It was also Sontag who noted that the notorious photographs of the concentration camps – showing emaciated corpses stacked like cordwood, and the survivors: living skeletons with grotesquely swollen heads – were inerrant in the extreme. When the camps were working, the process was expeditious: there were no piles lying around – just *Arbeit* then the ovens. That this: the testimony to the most pitiless of inhumanities still within the darkening purview of human memory should itself be irredeemably partial, is surely the only confirmation we need that photography is the medium not consequent upon, or conditional for the postmodern, but entwined in it.

A convolvulus – for in the age of motion capture, facial recognition and the ubiquitous handheld bidirectional computer-cum-camera, these technologies have twined the actual and the virtual, such that everyone sees in a glass brightly – even as they stumble in a dark wood. Because 'Then came film,' as Walter Benjamin near-phatically remarks 'and burst this prison-world asunder by the dynamite of the tenth of the second.' Collins might, quite reasonably, quibble with the calibration – one tenth of a second doesn't actually correspond to any either particularly pregnant, or practicable period in photography – but not, I suspect, with the sentiment. It's no accident that his own lens is angled towards things that will endure, while his own exposition focuses on images that already have.

Under such circumstances – all civic space a battleground, beset by the rat-a-tat-tat of skeuomorphic shutters – how can it be possible to redeem the image, and to wrest it once more from this welter? The answer is, of course, that the receiver of the image, quite as much as its taker, must abide with it. Just as all writers must be readers, so all photographers should be viewers of them. And I'm not talking about super-recognisers of their own lust, who, like those called in to help detectives sift through tens of thousands of suspects, can spot the pre-criminal on Tinder or Grinder or Whatever, who will break their heart.

Collins makes the case for photography as a revitalisation of portraiture – not its death by a billion selfies. The portraiture he wishes for, though, is ideally interpersonal: and in the amateur family photographs of the mid-twentieth century (surely, non-coincidentally, his own childhood), he finds this quality of lens and eye regarding one another with an affection at once revelatory and guarded. The unique prints matter as well – yes, the negatives are still there, tucked in the opposite pocket of the wallet, but let's face it (and face the skull in the garden at the same time), no one's ever going to develop another print of Aunt Maisie at Morecambe Bay, August, 1964.

Except for Collins – who in abiding with these revenants, demands we, too, abide with the irrealism of these images of the past, while accepting it's the closest we'll ever get to the reality of perception. 'The artist,' McLuhan avers, 'is an expert in sense-perception.' On that basis alone, Collins is an artist – on the basis of these essays, he's manifestly a writer as well.

– Coronation Day, Tenby –

The copperplate script in the tiled doorway spells SQUIBBS in letters the size of a man's shoe. An archetypal Edwardian shopfront with a pair of plate glass windows and a heavy glass door, Squibbs was the kind of photography shop found in almost every British town. It had a red-and-white awning and a yellow Kodak sign. Once a beacon of promise for holiday photographs, like memories of summers long gone, its colours and meaning have faded over the years. The day I visited, Squibbs was on the verge of closing; its neon-lit interior was as lifeless as a morgue. On the red baize of the main display case were two amateur flash guns, decades old with discoloured price tags. Between them lay a shiny booklet showing a colour photograph of a woman with backlit hair. Mirrored shelving lined the glazed cabinets on the walls. A cheerful girl with a pink ribbon in her hair still smiled out from the adverts for Colour Care enlargements, but the party had ended long ago. Pallid cardboard boxes presented a variety of exposure meters and flash bulbs that would never see the light of an exposure. Perfectly good cameras in greying vinyl cases languished unused, solemn reminders of yesterday's eager promises. Spread around the shelves and walls were photographs of weddings, parties, children and babies, landscapes and sunsets and dogs. Old black-and-white photographs had given way to vibrant prints, the earliest of which had a magenta hue, while newer impersonal portraits with bubble-gum backdrops elbowed out the past.

The owner, Graham Hughes, was a kindly-faced man in his seventies who I'd known for about fifteen years. Gesturing towards the back of the shop, he told me about the darkroom he used to have and the equipment he had installed there, equipment which he had tried and failed to give away to a college. He showed me some postcards he had made from his photographs of local views. Shuffling through a dozen or so examples of a particular scene, he inspected his work from decades ago, each print slightly differing in brightness and contrast. The picture was of a wide, sandy beach under a billowing cloudy sky, dark headlands night-black in shadow under the glare of the sun, and in the middle foreground, tiny but discernible figures, a man and woman, out walking along the beach, struggling towards the light.

Stuck on the wall behind Graham was a black-and-white photocopy of a group photograph of about a hundred people gathered on the side of a hill. Thinking it would make an ideal gift for a friend of mine who collects group photos, I asked him whether I could buy a small print of this picture. He explained that it was

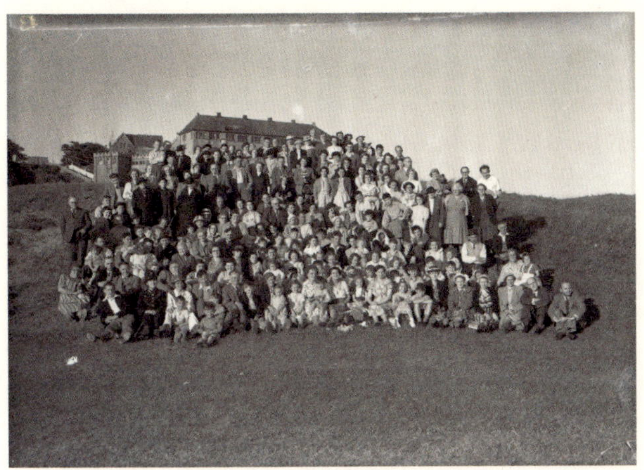

Graham Hughes, *Coronation Day, Tenby, 1953*

too difficult for him to provide reprints, but took the photograph down and placed it on the counter. Photographed in bright sunshine, its details were obscured by the sooty shadows of the heavily contrasting tones. An unexceptional photograph without obvious compositional merit, the photocopy showed it at its worst. Underneath the picture, CORONATION DAY, TENBY was written in biro. Graham smoothed out the slightly curled paper with the palm of his hand. 'I took that on the golf links near Shanley's.' Built in 1929, Shanley's South Beach Pavilion had a dance hall, a skating rink, an amusement arcade, a roof garden, and a cinema, which had shown the first talkie in Tenby. Graham had joined a group that tried to prevent the council demolishing the building, but it was leveled in 1981. He had taken the photograph on a half-plate camera, and still had the glass negative. He spoke wistfully about the range of tones that could be printed from the negative, and wished he could show me a proper print of the picture. 'Photography was photography in those days.'

After searching through several drawers, Graham found the glass negative in a glassine sleeve. Gently holding the brittle paper in his left hand, he pinched the edge of the glass with his finger tips and carefully slid it out of its wrapper, placing the negative face down. The photographic emulsion, an oleaginous coating of black and umber and silver, covered the negative save for a thin margin of bare glass at the selvage. We both leant closer to see the light on it from different angles, looking at what lay within the reflective surface of the emulsion. Only a partial aspect of the negative image was visible at any one time, as the light caught a facet of the picture in its silver membrane, vanishing back within its depths before another aspect surfaced.

One of the corners was cracked and held together with Sellotape. There was a long scratch running along the top, and a little piece of emulsion had been chipped off. When Graham held it up to the light, we could see that the exposure had been technically sound; it would yield a superb print. I told him that I had a flat-bed scanner, which could bring out all the nuances and details, and he offered to lend it to me. After replacing the negative in its sleeve, he rummaged in another drawer for a shallow cardboard box, into which he carefully packed the negative. I was struck by the kindness and trust that he was showing a complete stranger, and assured him that I would take great care of his glass negative and would make a high-quality print for him. All he asked was that I return the negative to him by hand. Then, following the old procedure, he took out a ledger from under the counter and passed it to me to write down my name and address. I shook his hand and left, the shop bell dinging me on my way.

Initially, I made a low-resolution scan to give me an overview. Immediately a fuller picture emerged, the amorphous crowd blossoming into an assembly of individually distinct people. The sky, cloudless blue on the day, is rendered in a uniform tone of featureless pale grey. Such is technology, the scan highlights its flaws forensically, tearing the fabric of realism's artifice. The scratch along the top appears as a vicious scar, accentuated by its proximity to a dark band in the sky, an effect caused by uneven development during the film's processing. A series of faint vertical streaks transforms Tenby's sky into a backdrop, and a nebula of blotches and circles and scratches, overlain with a constellation of black dots, swathes the grey yonder. On the grass, the chip in the emulsion pokes a white hole in the realism, interjecting antimatter into the Tuesday afternoon. Just above the cracked bottom corner, a purple stain on the grass adds alien colour, as does an inverted letter B in the top left of the sky,

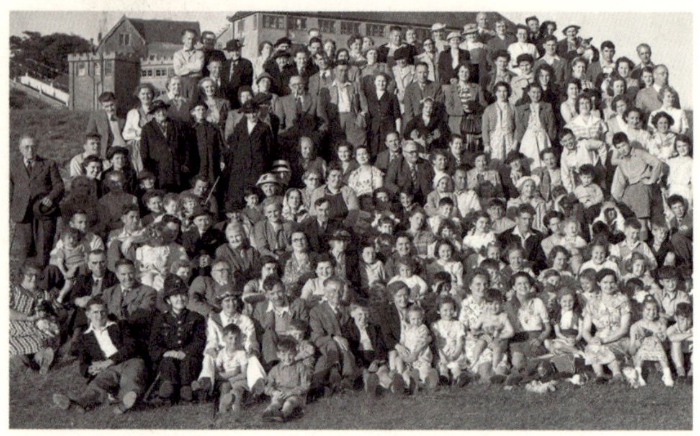

Graham Hughes, *Coronation Day, Tenby, 1953* (detail)

forming a yellow bundle of curves floating out of the frame.

Sharply defined in the bright sunshine against the scrim of the sky, the crowd of people clustered together have a more pronounced presence than all of the other elements, which have a softer definition. The pallid midtones of the anaemic grass and blanched buildings consign these features to the periphery, while the ranks of residents, their place in the light affirmed by the black of their shadows, congregate in the epicentre, as they stare out at the camera in a spectrum from ebony to off-white and every shade of grey. The late afternoon sunshine rakes across them diagonally, leaving the pitch of their shadows trailing behind them in a celestial breeze. Depending on the light, photography's realism can be unworldly, emphatic in its notation, severe in its demarcation. To the naked eye, a shadow is a puddle whose surface can be seen through; to a camera, in strong sunlight, it's a fathomless crevasse. The shadows in the picture head off to the top right corner, where the knoll ends precipitously with a fringe of stubbly grass and nothing but blank grey. On the left-hand side of the picture, the buildings and trees ground the scene in everyday life, but the emptiness of the opposite corner is as vacant and unnerving as the horizon on the moon.

Crowning the left side of the hill, Shanley's western façade faces the afternoon sun. Running along the upper floor of the turn-of-the-century building, a row of closely spaced windows keeps watch on the events below. Further along to the left, standing slightly behind its dominant neighbour, sits a squat concrete building with a castellated roofline, its incongruity mocked by the triad of drainpipes splayed across its south-western wall. Beyond that, ablaze in the afternoon sunlight, a grand flight of white steps with lamp posts proudly ascends an embankment. Two lines of bunting flap in the breeze, their white pennants singing out in the sunshine against the wild verdancy of a mature tree in the background. Emerging in an open space between two trees, the top of the steps is flanked on the near side by an advertising hoarding, in front of which a seated figure on a bench observes the scene below. At the edge of the picture, its glass panels glistening, is a telephone box.

Gathered together that June day are the residents

of Harris Street and Trafalgar Street, corralled in front of the camera for their Coronation Day photograph. By the hour of their sundial's shadows, the day's celebrations were already well underway. The costumes of two women sitting in the front on the left, one a policeman, the other wearing a sash and a Union Jack bonnet, suggest that there had been a pageant. Sitting among his friends on the other side of the group is a little boy with a blacked-up face. This picture is that afternoon's afterwards; the Union Jacks are droopy in the children's hands. The tight arrangement of seated children and adults in the front rows unravels in the lines of people standing behind them. It is a feat of marshalling on the part of the photographer, and testimony to the patience, or obedience, of the children waiting at the front. Graham would have called out for their attention and stillness, claiming their concentration. This is the moment when they composed themselves, when the camera holds its breath, as they entrust the light of their presence into the silver embrace of the photograph.

To look at the photograph even more closely, I rescan the negative at a far greater resolution. The scanner grinds away and then the screen comes to life with a deeper, richer, more highly defined image. The larger scan makes it possible to zoom in further and further until their faces are enlarged to the size of a plum, and from the impersonal ranks, individuals emerge, each a singular face in a crowd. Lit from behind in the glow of the computer, the image of a small section fills the screen, welling up out of the past. The original photograph is suddenly brought to life, like the shock of hearing the recording of a long lost voice. The crowd's anonymity falls like a cloak, exposing each individual in turn. To look through the camera's eye is to be faced with those people looking straight back. As I zoom in on them, so they loom out at me with all the psychological intensity of their look all those decades ago, as direct now as it was then.

There is something eerie about seeing them so closely; looking at the way they faced the camera, the shadows and lines on their faces, the shape of their mouths, as they held still and focused on the lens. People whose names I have never known, have never met; inhabitants of a pair of streets that I have neither seen nor walked. They would never have thought that seventy years later, using technology that did not exist in their day, a complete stranger would be peering into their faces. They would have assumed that only close friends and family would ever see this photograph. Zooming in so far that fifteen faces fill the screen, each responds in their own way to that afternoon's sunshine, each a member of the group photograph's cast. Enlarged to this degree, the negative's emulsion becomes apparent, so the photograph appears overlain with a patina of the film's grain, an ectoplasm separating their reality from ours, a material reminder of the picture's photochemical fabrication. By looking past

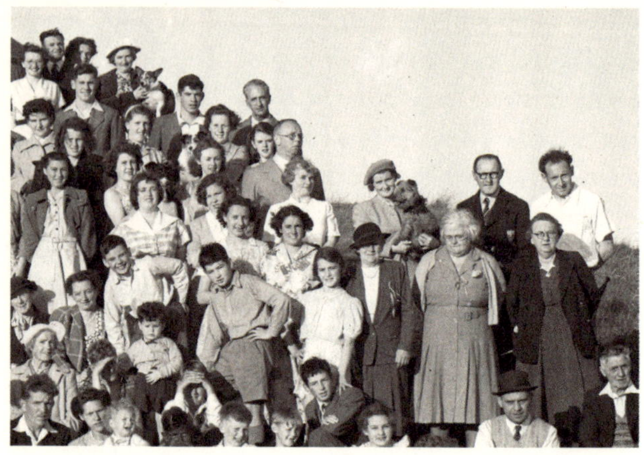

Graham Hughes, *Coronation Day, Tenby, 1953* (detail)

the photograph's grain into its metaphysicality, the picture's meaning comes alive, like type turning into words, words into ideas.

More anarchy than military, they form an unruly semi-circle. The little children sit on the ground in the front, while the people behind stand in a series of fan-shaped lines. Weaving around the gentle slope, the rows snake from side to side, leaving some people almost obscured behind friends and siblings. There must be more than two hundred. Most of those in the first row have their legs stretched out in front of them with the soles of their shoes sticking up at right angles. This and the effect of the camera's perspective, which foreshortens their legs, makes them appear formal and comical, a look so characteristic of a British summer fête. Typically, the weather, while sunny, is not warm.

It rained in London on Coronation Day. Some brave the day in cottons, others resort to woollens. On the very end of the back row, on the windward side of the group, a cigarette in his mouth, arms wrapped around him to keep warm, stands a man in shirt sleeves; the breeze has caught his lapel, which flaps up against his face, like a cold wind on a cat's coat.

Barely half a decade after the war, many of the men are wearing demob suits. Some fit better than others; outsized shoulders hang loosely, folds of cloth sag like downturned smiles. Austerity Britain and clothing coupons were a few summers past, and the bright new future promised a new dawn, but the neon lights of consumerism were still blinking awake. Looking back through the rear-view mirror of Brexit Britain at the country a lifetime ago, it is all too easy, and too facile, to draw sketchy conclusions based on the clothes and expressions these people wore one memorable afternoon. The man in the lower right corner in a tie, shirt sleeves and pullover, looks like he is wearing a hat that is too small, sitting as it does above his ears. But zooming in, averting the man's gaze which bores out of the picture, his hat, a Homburg, might instead be tilted slightly back, showing his whole face to the camera. Towards the back on the left, tanned and handsome in an easy smile, is a confident man wearing a suit and waistcoat – the Full Monty in post-war parlance. With his wayward fringe blown across his forehead, his tie raffishly loose, he appears untroubled, his confidence making him look like a character from a cigarette advert. Or so it seems, caught in that light for that fraction of a second.

Apart from the older ones who are wearing hats, nearly all the women have their hair in the same home-styled permanent wave. So prized were curls, children with wavy hair wear it long. Like the women, older men wear hats, younger ones not. The older women wear long woollen coats, maintaining appearances and warmth on that chilly afternoon. Midway up on the first row of standing figures are four elderly ladies in dark coats and hats, black as rooks. One stands slightly in front of the other three, who appear to defer to her assumed status. Her black, broad-brimmed hat has a wide ribbon on which is pinned an H-shaped brooch which glints in the light. The cloth of her Edwardian coat drapes loosely over her elderly frame. A figure from the previous century, like her three friends, she had lived through two world wars. All four are unaccompanied by men. Shaded by the brim of her hat, her hooded eyes regard the camera with a censorious look. Whether this is how she looked at life, or merely how she addressed that camera, remains conjecture.

In brighter clothes and faces, the children beam out from the front. Seated with them are four middle-aged women and an older man, shepherding the children like teachers, which is presumably what they are. The older man, the headmaster, immaculately turned out in a suit and tie and turn-ups, smiles in a grandfatherly manner. Two of his colleagues have children on their laps. Sitting straight upright between them is a slightly older girl in a smart new dress. Fastidious and ostensibly well-behaved, she would be easy to cast as the goody-goody alongside the boys in crumpled shirts. One boy, with the long arm of the headteacher around his shoulder, is decked out in a jacket and shorts with a shirt and jumper, but his attire is undermined by the spike sitting up in his hair, and utterly undone by his little brother's cheeky face. To the right of the headmaster, easily within his reach, are twins in matching shirts. One sits slightly in front, smiling, while his brother sits behind him, frowning. Next to the headmaster is another man with his arm around a boy. He is leaning into the camera, trying his best in a fatherly way. It is presumptuous, but irresistible, to read tiny narratives in the picture; stories that come from our lives, not theirs. Social history is inflected by personal history; a broader history, a collective memory, condenses into experience and introspection. My brother and I had those same flannel shirts, and I smiled like that, and he grimaced like that, and when he was able, my father leaned into the picture too. If only I had turned around. The owl of Minerva flies at dusk. Photography's gift comes with despair. The ship in the picture has sailed; what you can see now you were not able to have seen then.

Coronation Day was of an era when Viyella was a fabric, not merely a brand, and Britain still had a wool and cotton industry. Wafting from those two hundred heartbeats on the hillside that afternoon, above the smell of Players and Old Spice, was the fug of old woollens exhaled from warm bodies. Sniffing the air, muzzling into the occasion, are a Corgi, a Welsh terrier, a spaniel and a couple of other mutts. High up on the back row, ears and nose like a propeller, the Corgi is held up in the crook of its owner's arm. A rosy-cheeked woman in a summer hat and winter coat, she tries to point the Corgi towards the camera, but her dog is distracted by the spaniel down on the far side, whose owner, jovial-faced in glasses and a jaunty dress, struggles to hold her dog while trying to sit upright and smile, a lost cause as the spaniel is overcome by an enormous yawn. A couple of rows below the Corgi, shoulder high, is a Collie with a white patch on one side of its face. The owner, her wavy hair surfing the breeze, looks straight into the camera, her face a picture of happiness. As is the teenager standing below her, oblivious of the dog's nose behind her. She is probably more conscious of the old black-and-white dog panting over her right shoulder. The owner of the black-and-white dog looks as though she could be the younger woman's mother; even with the dog between them, they stand close to one another as if in a pair, both in summer dresses. Lit by the sun, the daughter's face (if indeed she is the daughter) holds youth and promise and a new future, while her mother's eyes seem to have a wariness and unease. Whether this is the consequence of a troubled history (they appear unaccompanied by a husband and father), or the effort of trying to keep their dog under control, or simply a lapse in composure as the lens opened, it is impossible to tell, for the members of a photograph are elective mutes.

I have a high-quality print made from the scan of the negative, nearly four times the size of the photocopy in Squibbs. It is not a conventionally beautiful photograph but a picture of beauty. The grass in the foreground appears vague and lifeless. The camera's focus is concentrated on the people, who are depicted so sharply in relation to the rest of the picture, it is as though they have alighted in this particular place and time, which in some respects they have. Together, they constitute a performance, an act of social realist theatre, individuals presenting themselves as a whole. Close your eyes, allow them time to disassemble, and the production has vanished into the afternoon. The picture's formal properties are relatively bland, although the velvety tones of all the blacks and greys have that tactile appeal characteristic of a vintage silver gelatine print. Physically, it is almost unrecognisable from the photocopy. Holding the print by the window to examine it in daylight reveals the full range of tones; the deep blacks in the elderly ladies' dark coats, the dark greys in the shadows of the men's lighter suits and the soft palette of the women's cardigans. A large negative produces an almost oily depth, accentuating the shapes of their faces and the hang of their clothes. It is as though you can not only hear every nuance in the recording, but the sound of the sound of the recording. But it lacks the puddles of silver in the darkest parts that appear in older prints; there is no metal in a digital print (and possibly no iron in its soul). This print was never held by any of the people in the picture; it has not aged with them; it was produced as a print of our time, not theirs. Technically it is superior, but it is Netflix, not home movie. Higher production values strain authenticity: something is missing.

Compared to the ability to zoom in further and further to the scan on screen, using a magnifying glass to look more closely into the picture only takes you so far. But extreme digital scrutiny produces a falsely forensic examination. Zoomed in to one hundred percent magnification, the photograph's details are expanded to the point of distortion; the grain of the film makes the spaniel's tongue exactly the same texture as the woman's skin. This degree of enlargement releases the tiniest details – the glint in the dog's eye, the woman's teeth – but overlays them with a freckled film, depersonalising the picture into the texture of a billboard. The print has all the same details, but at arm's length, welling up in the roving sphere of the magnifying glass, whereas the massively enlarged scan breaks the spell, replacing wonder with interrogation. The print, in comparison, speaks in a soft voice which must be listened to carefully, and at a respectable distance, upholding the integrity of the optical imprint in silver. The limits of what is revealed must be respected.

As our lives are informed by a penumbral awareness, so a photograph is framed by its context, which in this particular case is written in biro. Whether in ink, gilt lettering or the solemn voice of a Buckingham Palace commentator, such occasions are steeped in all those invisibles taken for granted: the Royal Family, the Home Service, National Service, two world wars, Great Britain in the epicentre of the globe. Above the birdsong, the children's whispers and their parents' shushes, the strains of *Rule Britannia* drift over the Tenby hillside. According to the photograph's unequivocal version, there was not a single person of colour among the inhabitants of Tenby's Harris and Trafalgar Streets. But photography is an unreliable witness. It speaks with resolute confidence and clarity; this is how it was. To draw on the Russian proverb, photography lies like an eyewitness. A photograph does not acknowledge what preceeded or followed the exposure. It admits only what is shown. Whatever there was just outside of the frame – arbitrarily, deliberately or from another angle – apparently does not exist. The photograph is its sole account, its truth set in silver stone. It is a form of memorial, and like all memorials, it demonstrates a particular truth. Quite how, and to what extent, that chosen truth is transcribed from the rays of light has a long and evasive history.

The almost magical property of photography, the

reason why it was initially greeted with such astonishment, is that a photograph shows a much more detailed view of the subject, desired or otherwise, than the observer could possibly have envisaged. Opening the lens is like opening the bottle and letting the genie of light expose itself on the film, recording a welter of unrestrained information. Everything is swept up, from stray wisps of hair to worn soles, creased collars to frown lines. In its very essence, photography is not only bluntly direct but feral. True to life, it is complex and messy and beyond simplistic interpretation. It lingers on the way we present ourselves, registering details that we might hope would go unseen, or at least unremarked, and alights on them. It is the awkward voice behind self-image, showing the face that others see, not the one in our imaginations. Doubts, insecurities and ill-fitting jackets, the photograph picks up on them all. Vulnerabilities and inadequacies can be presented implacably, or emphasised by harsh light, or distorted in jaundiced angles. A narrowing of the eyes can look shifty, suspicious, or mean, when in reality, it might just be a squint. A trick of the light can cast a spell on an otherwise innocent scene. As with prose, photography's equivalent of clear thinking and writing is calm composure.

Ultimately, photography is the art of looking. Suspending judgement and looking closely, further and further into the picture, letting preconceptions come and go. Listening very closely, hearing the silences as much as the sounds, listening with all of the senses. It is often said that the mark of great art is that it shows you the world in a new light, but surely the measure of great art is that it shows you the world more profoundly. Photography is the art that stops still and looks closely. All of the novel possibilities of photography – its previously unimaginably complex depiction; the freezing of motion; the forms of shadows; its agency in the Machine Age, and so forth – are predicated on observation.

Photography's ubiquity is its nemesis. Omnipresent, louder and dumber, increasingly simplistic, airbrushed of nuance, uncertainty and ambiguity, most of what we are served up as photography is the antithesis of photography itself. *Coronation Day, Tenby* is an inimitable imprint of life, and if photography was viewed carefully, rather than superficially, then its perceptive (hence artistic) value would be more recognised and its true depths plumbed. It would also demolish the false dichotomy between 'personal' photography and 'professional'. If people did take pictures in their gardens that looked like ones from *National Geographic* then it really would be the end of the world. Equally, post-modernism has no relevance when people are looking at their own personal pictures.

Of course, there is an aesthetic dimension, as there are other socio-political elements and cultural references bearing on the picture, but these are peripheral. At its core are all those personal threads secreted in the picture, the *madeleines* we can sense, the neural pathways they arouse. It might be because family photography can be so awkward and embarrassing that the 'professional' stance is to stamp on anything with the slightest suspicion of sentimentality and treat it coldly and impersonally. Nothing vulnerable, nothing gained. Mindfulness and introspection do not equal solipsism, just as ostentatious intellectualising is not the same as wisdom. By ultimately taking the picture personally, by venturing beyond form and comparison, using theory as a vehicle rather than a terminus, opens unconstrained and unforeseen possibilities.

There is, of course, a massive difference between a group photograph of some Welsh citizens and a photograph of your own family. Rather than a sunny Tenby hillside, family photographs are flowerbeds with landmines. Nothing is as personal as family, but nothing human is alien to other people, and so exploring this photograph, passing through these peoples' lives at this particular moment in time, is passing through a part of all of our lives, too. As I look further into the picture, so I can see further into my own past. The sunshine faces are interspersed with doubt. Some people look troubled, uncomfortable at the prospect of being seen, not wishing their look to be on record. I salute the people holding up their dogs, and would like to be like them, and can be on good days, but I am drawn to the boy at the back of the seated section who looks a little unsure of what is going on, or how he should be. Or the teenager on the right-hand side of the group, sitting next to his brother. His brother's face stares out at the camera, but he is almost hidden behind an old lady in a straw hat, and he stands slightly to the side, partly to keep the sun out of his eyes, partly to avoid the light. Looking through my lens, he is not so at home in the photograph, and possibly not so at home in the world. The prism of retrospection bends light through complicated angles.

It is too easy and knowing to dismiss family portraits as personal propaganda. Taken on sunny days and smart ones, it is said that these kinds of photographs offer, at best, a partial truth, at worst, a deceitful one, plastering over the cracks. But photography is far more complicated than that, as are we, and as is our relationship with photography. For every photograph of a happy Christmas, there are many more tinged with unhappiness. Within a generation of its invention, portrait photography had become commonplace, and consciously and instinctively, people can perceive extremely subtle nuances in photographs of themselves, nuances evident in photographs of others too. This might be because of the primal significance of developing facial recognition in infancy, the mirroring of parental observation and attention. Babies like looking at people's faces and are capable of recognising their parents and primary carers by the time they are only two weeks old. Humans' capacity for interpreting facial expressions is an innate and genetically determined ability, honed by *Homo habilis* onwards. Maybe this is one reason why most people will confidently and quickly distinguish between a 'good' and a 'bad' photograph of themselves or someone they know, an emphatic judgement made with alacrity, an incontrovertible truth. And once upon a time and happy ever after. People spend their whole lives searching for truths, and the more certain they are about them, the more fragile they are.

Photography's apparent realism makes it the most accessible, understandable and credible of all the visual arts. People relate instinctively to photography. It has the uncontrived eloquence of directly recorded experience; that raw expression of humanity, so potent in transcribed forms such as oral history, leaves fingerprints in the photograph's profusion of incidental detail. The voice and vernacular of oral history, the combination of the ostensibly important and superfluous, are what makes it so compellingly believable and informative. Photography takes this to an extreme degree because it has no filter; everything and anything is recorded indifferently. Incidental detail is the hallmark of photography. God is not in the details; everyday life is. The way the lady's pearl necklace hangs underneath the left lapel of her blouse. The mother's hand reaching through her daughter's arms, holding her close. The white ribbon worn by the girl with Down's syndrome, the stick attached to her little Union Jack that is slipping through her fingers;

her mother's striped dress under her heavy coat, the undulating leather of her handbag, the Box Brownie camera in her hands.

Possibly it is because people are so used to the notion of choosing one from a number of photographs that photography is seen as something that can be easily assessed, like a Victoria sponge in a village show. Rarely is such confidence expressed so readily in relation to painting, and it is generally believed that it takes longer to look at a painting than a photograph, which speaks volumes about how photography is regarded. Compared to photography, in painting and drawing, proportionately far more looking precedes the mark-making; in photography, the onus is retrospective. To paint is to make marks of intention; to photograph is to imprint observation. Photography arose from the superabundant details traced by hand in the *camera obscura*, the result of lengthy scrutiny – and even then, the agenda was to judiciously simplify. Once the draughtsman's paper had been replaced by photosensitive paper, that temporal process was reversed. Ease of use and human nature being what they are, speed of creation encourages speed of consumption. The further photography is divorced from its roots as a tripod-mounted apparatus originating from the *camera obscura*, the more it is shot from the hip or one hand, the more its fundamentals are overlooked.

Plurality is photography's Achilles' heel. The shutter release has a trigger for a button; held down, a volley of shots rings out. The cliché of the professional, like all clichés, containing a gold nugget of truth, is a photographer who shoots scores of frames, spraying the subject with hopeful possibilities to be edited afterwards. In a professional portrait session this might seem *de rigueur*, but person to person in everyday life, it would appear wanton, inept or insane. Fashion photography aside, a portrait is a visual understanding between the photographer and the subject, which is why ordinary people can make, and often take, the most perceptive portraits. Tellingly, all the finest portrait photographers that I know find that nearly always the best portrait is the one made in the first frame. Photography is a prisoner of seriality. Rarely is photography exhibited as a single picture, and yet without seeing each one as an individual, it can become muffled in the crowd, however pleasing the chorus. Photographs can play off one another with sensitive sequencing and curating, bringing out motifs and meanings that might otherwise be more mute, but each must be viewed in its inimitable uniqueness.

When photography was invented, it was assumed that it would be as much a means of reproducing images as a unique method of creating them. Photography's dilemma is whether it is an object or a medium; although its essence is based on the art of fixing a shadow, the nature of its actual existence remains shadowy. With the exception of the daguerreotype, the single image photograph that has no negative, a photograph has no original form; it is a sequence of processes. In analogue photography, the negative is the primordial, but it is an 'antepicture', a mould awaiting a cast. In the nineteenth century, when it was not yet possible to register a bright sky and a dark landscape on a single exposure, it was customary to make two and combine them in the printing, forming a photograph of dual origin. Contemporary technology has made it possible to print photographs to almost any size and to bring to light an even wider spectrum of tones and shades from within the negative's emulsion or the camera's sensor; digitally, the possibilities are almost infinite. Countless sequential digital exposures can be registered, expanding the optical range way beyond the relatively small spectrum of its analogue ancestor. Similarly, the depth of field can be elongated from the foreground to the background by sandwiching a series of exposures with staggered focus. Between the negative or sensor and the projection or print, it is uncertain where lies the photograph. A print of a photograph, commonly regarded as its form, is merely one iteration, and the print can take many forms in terms of condition and size, weight and tone, and form of printing.

Each manifestation, be it on a wall, a page, a screen or in the hand, has its distinct qualities and nuances. Of all the plastic arts, it is the most elastic. The over-whelming majority of digital photography is only ever viewed on a screen, be it a monitor or a phone, and never takes form as a physical object. The physicality of a tableau-sized photograph is a wholly different creature to the dog-eared miniature in a wallet. An immersive and physically interactive experience, a large print on a wall requires the viewer to move in relation to the picture, placing spatial demands on the spectator, while the smaller print can be handled, the viewer able to move it around in the light, and if unmounted, to place a lamp behind it, and through this rear projection, not unlike the light within a computer screen, unmask the details lurking in the shadows, uncovering aspects that the tableau print lays bare at scale.

There is a palpable difference between looking at the print of *Coronation Day*, holding the physical photograph up to the light, the illumination bathed in its rich tones, the people's faces levitating in the lens of the magnifying glass, to the intangible, untethered, expanding and contracting backlit scan on the screen. The digital is forever beyond the grasp of touch, that naïve grope at understanding. Whereas the scar tissue on the negative is explicit in the scan, it disfigures the corporeality of the print; old wounds on an elderly body. The immateriality of the screen image exists in a parallel universe to the optical imprint in Tenby. The fleeting nature of that afternoon disappears with the light; only afterwards, all too late, are looks and words and gestures seen wistfully. As the magnifying glass glides over the print, discrete circles of life emerge and recede, their presence heightened and then sunk back into the folds of the photograph. The scan can pick their words apart but permits no cross-examination. They lie sealed within the print as though beneath an invisible sheet of glass, the pane of the past through which nothing can pass. Ours is not the last word. Stubbornly, the print allows only so much magnification; the scan can expand into atoms. In the print, the figures remain rooted in their late afternoon light, but illuminated on screen, if pressed too hard, their presence loses definition and becomes transparent, blending into the grain of the emulsion, evaporating into the crepuscular light. But all photography is beyond touch and grasp, for it is a trace of a projection, and the essence of it lies between the two.

As an object, the newly printed, pristine version of *Coronation Day* is a reproduction of the past. And yet the light that passed through the negative's emulsion on the scanner follows exactly the same imprint as the light that passed through the camera's lens that day. To view the picture is to look through the same aperture as that lens, standing in the tripod's shoes, the viewer's gaze meeting those of the people who stare back. Just as the camera's lens summoned them to look straight at it, the photograph demands the same of the viewer. To truly look at a photograph like this, to look at the actual 'lightprints' of their lives in the instant of the photograph, that second of their breathing presence, is to hear the roar that lies behind the photograph's silence. To look deeply is to form a bond with the picture; even though they are dead and gone, the viewer enters into their lives. *Soavemente disse ch'io posasse.* The man in the Homburg and shirt sleeves is looking straight at the lens, directly at us. His dark eyebrows form a black shade over his eyes. He sits slightly apart from the people around him, and his gaze is piercing.

– A Big Hairy Hand –

Like a lot of good ideas, it started off the wrong way round. In the summer of 1992, London Zoo was facing a catastrophic cut in funding. At the time, I was the picture editor of the *Telegraph Magazine*. Every Tuesday afternoon, we would sit in the editor's office, eating sandwiches, having a meeting to discuss prospective ideas. Talk turned to the future of the zoo. Cynicism being the currency of those conversations, one journalist wondered what on earth divorced dads might do with their children on weekends were the zoo to close. This led to a suggestion, popularly received, that the magazine should commission a photographer to take ironic black-and-white photographs of families visiting the zoo. My response was that this was a dog-eared idea that had been done repeatedly. What if we got the chimpanzees to take photographs of the public? I was laughed out of the meeting. All the way back to my desk, where I got on the telephone to the zoo.

The head keeper, Mick Carman, listened in silence to my request and replied that, actually, it was an interesting idea because the chimpanzees are intelligent and get bored. In the wild they use twigs as primitive tools to retrieve termites, etc. from rotten trees, an activity that the zoo would try to replicate by placing nuts inside specially hollowed logs, giving the chimps little bamboo sticks that they could use to poke through the holes to get at the food. 'Behaviour enrichment' was the term he used. As long as it was safe and the chimpanzees could not hurt themselves, he welcomed the idea. So, a few days later we met at the zoo. I brought along Tim O'Sullivan, a professional portrait photographer, to help with the technical practicalities and know-how. The tongue-in-cheek conceit was to mimic a magazine portrait set up with a Hasselblad camera. The cardinal rule was that we had to keep back from their cage and ensure the chimpanzees could not reach any piece of equipment because they would likely swallow it and choke. He stressed how aggressive and dangerous they are. 'Think of them as football hooligans.'

Stereotyped as circus performers, *Pan troglodytes* are an endangered species. Facing habitat loss, poaching and disease, less than a third of a million survive in the wild. Although chimpanzees and humans share 98.7% of their DNA sequence, we have used them for food, entertainment, laboratory experiments and astronauts. We have taught them a rudimentary sign language, even though they have their own. Weighing as much as seventy kilograms, pound for pound, adult males are twice as strong as humans.

After a bit of trial and error, we worked out the following system, thanks in large part to Tim

O'Sullivan's assistant, Gavin Burke, who took over the practical side of the photography by focusing the camera, adjusting the exposure and changing rolls of film. Separating the chimpanzees' steel enclosure from the waist-high metal barriers that kept the public back, was a six-foot-wide *cordon sanitaire* with a prickly hedge. We placed the tripod-mounted Hasselblad in a gap in the bushes, shielded behind a large wooden board. Mounted above the camera was a long, slim log with a hole drilled through the middle, into which the button of the camera's cable release was threaded and then smeared with banana. The idea was that the chimps would poke at the banana with little bamboo sticks, unknowingly pressing the cable release's button. To make it look as though the photographs showed what the view was like from inside their enclosure, a section of the same steel mesh was mounted in front of the camera.

Come the day, there was a television crew, a few zookeepers, a journalist and a cage full of indignant chimpanzees. As it was mid-morning, there were relatively few visitors and our Wallace and Gromit set-up looked rather pitiful. We marked a big X on the path, focused the camera to this distance and displayed a large, optimistic sign proclaiming: HAVE YOUR PORTRAIT TAKEN BY A CHIMPANZEE! Immediately, groups of school children milled around, wondering what was going on. Meanwhile the chimps started barracking us: they knew a huckster when they saw one. I tried to corral the school kids to the spot where the camera was focused, but the more they pushed and teased each other, unsure whether they were being set up, the more riotous the primates became. The kids made monkey faces at the chimps and the chimps made monkey faces at the kids and everyone screamed.

Mick Carman had warned us darkly about how dangerous the chimps could be: if you put a finger through the grille, it would be torn off. When Gavin stepped up to their cage to check the camera (under the hawk-like supervision of a zookeeper), the chimpanzees became apoplectic, throwing themselves at the mesh, hanging onto it and shaking the grille with ear-splitting screams. You could feel their breath. A keeper threw some bamboo sticks into the cage. The chimps immediately picked them up, and either chewed them or cleaned their ears with them, but their attention remained fixed on the camera, which seemed an affront to their dignity and was the target of their wrath. They clung to the grille, howling in gleeful frenzy. The kids went wild. One of the large female chimpanzees leapt up to the enclosure's ceiling and hung there from one hand, egged on by the others. Mick Carman pulled me away to the side. Everyone stared and waited to see what she was going to do. She cupped her other hand under her arse and crapped in it. We all fell about laughing. Mick pulled me further back. Suddenly, she cranked her arm back and chucked the steaming crap straight at the public, hitting a woman in a beige mac with a loud thwack, knocking her over. The chimps went berserk, laughing and screaming and jumping up and down, as two zookeepers helped the woman to her feet and took her away to be hosed down.

It was downhill from there. The chimps gradually lost interest, as did the television crew, and members of the public came and went, disappointed. Eventually the journalist, who was paid to attend, went home. The only ones left with any spirit were the chimpanzees, intermittently taunting us. Mick Carman was there at the end, helping us to clear up. Ruefully acknowledging that it had not worked, I could not help muttering something about how, in principle, it had been such a good idea. 'What about asking them?' he asked, gesturing to the adjacent enclosure. I turned to look and saw a huge gorilla, sitting on his haunches, calmly stroking his chin, and then looked back at our chimpanzees, who were giving us the finger. 'Tomorrow?'

The next day, minus the television crew, we set up the camera in front of the gorillas. We were accompanied by their keeper, Linda DaVolls. She had red hair, green eyes and smelt faintly of ape shit. The gorillas seemed to recognise her as she pointed them out to us. Kumba, twenty-four years old and twenty-five stone, was a male Silverback; Zaire was an eighteen-year-old female; and Salome a sixteen-year-old female, with a four-year-old daughter, Asali. Kumba dominated the others; a male Silverback gorilla is almost two metres

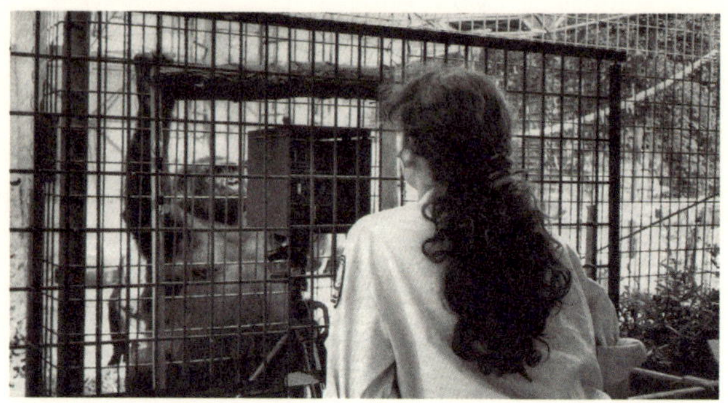

Michael Collins, *Linda DaVolls and Salome,* 1992

tall, weighs up to 270 kilograms, and has the strength of twenty men.

Linda plucked some bamboo shoots that were growing nearby and fed a few into their enclosure. Kumba picked one up, knuckle-walked over to the camera, peered at the apparatus and then sat down. Linda explained that the others would wait for him to get out of the way before they would come over to investigate. But Kumba just sat there, chewing a stick, more idle than inquisitive. Unlike the previous day with the chimpanzees, the atmosphere was calm, even reverent. The gorillas were huge and ponderous. Sometimes one would get up and move suddenly, and even though we were all perfectly safe on our side of the cage, we would ripple back, slightly unnerved. They would look at you with solemn amber eyes.

The film was loaded, and banana was smeared over the hole. Some kids pressed forward warily, watching

Kumba. The massive Silverback crouched behind the camera, hogging the space, doing nothing. Occasionally he looked at us wearily, lost in thought. Or zoned out. The kids grew impatient. A few stared intently, but most of them were restless, and started to give up on the idea. After about five minutes, Kumba trudged off and then Salome approached. Great excitement. Salome picked up the stick and peered at the slim log with the banana-filled hole. Rather than facing into the lens, we followed her movement with the stick. She held the thin bamboo very delicately between her finger and thumb, like a conductor's baton. The camera was about head height, but the hollowed-out branch was higher, and she had to reach up to poke the stick towards the banana. Because of the lines on their foreheads, gorillas look as though they are frowning with concentration. Salome's giant black hand held the stick motionlessly and then with the concentration of an electrician working on a fuse box, she pressed the stick into the aperture and to our amazement, the camera's shutter went click. The kids went crazy, wanting more. Gavin wound the film on. Salome licked the banana off the stick.

Rather than a decisive moment, there would be an indecisive interval, at times interminable, between clicks. Gorillas take their time. Our contraption was, at best, a distraction, and the reward of a teeny bit of mashed banana was little incentive to a group collectively weighing fifteen hundred pounds who had a

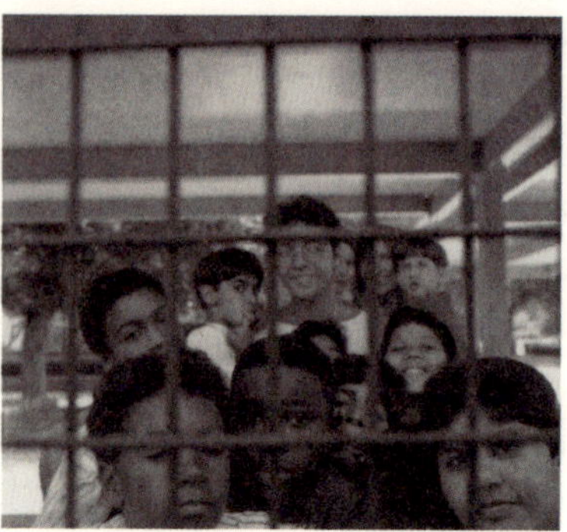

One of Salome's photographs

storage locker full of them out the back. It was less a matter of posing for the camera than waiting, and it was impossible to predict when the bamboo would trip the button under the banana. The more boisterous of the children, primed to make ape faces and noises, grew restless. So did most of the adults. You could wait five minutes for nothing to happen. The trauma of the previous day's shambles behind us, we thought we were on a roll, but most of the public came and went, disappointed by our sideshow. But by and large, the calm demeanor of the gorillas quietened people down, and unlike the chaotic chimps, the atmosphere was contemplative. Although some people reacted dismissively to the prospect of having to wait for the gorilla to get it together with the stick, to others this reversed the circus-like nature of the spectacle to one where we were literally waiting on the gorillas.

Even the gangs of schoolkids seemed put in their

place by the gorillas. They would start off laughing at the ape, pulling faces, trying to outdo each other, but their initial ridicule gradually ebbed away, replaced by inquisitiveness in the face of a gorilla standing behind a camera which was pointed at them. However preposterous the prospect, for some, a wonderful idea took shape in their minds. They would shove up against the grille and then grow quiet. Some faces gawped at the spectacle, not seeing a fellow creature, but others looked more gently, more sensitively. Parents would lift their little children up, holding them at eye-level to the gorilla, who would stand slowly taking in the scene in front of them.

A little girl with stick-thin arms and big ears leans as closely as possible into the lens, her wide eyes pools of wonder. Her face is framed by the grid of the grille, separating her mouth and jaw in one section, her nose, eyes and forehead in another, her left ear in a third. She peers in as intently as the chimpanzees had peered out, and has climbed onto the safety barrier, pressing forward as much as she dares. Her father, along with the other adults standing behind her, is looking above her, watching the gorilla with the bamboo stick as she pokes it near the cable release's button. While they seem absorbed by the process, and as her brother looks on with a frown, the little girl seems utterly drawn into the magical idea of having her picture taken by a gorilla.

The zoo was sparsely attended, and although people kept walking by, there were times when no one was around, so I would go off, looking for obliging folk to be photographed. A lot of people were initially wary, unsure what was going on, and worried that there might be a cost, financial or otherwise. Knowing even less then than I do now, I tried to find 'interesting-looking' people, as though some people are more interesting-looking than others. There was one particularly animated boy who seemed to be on his own. Fists clenched, bursting with energy and emotion, desperately wanting it to happen but doubting it would, every time he stood in front of the camera nothing happened, and he would take off, frustrated, pacing around nearby before coming back again for another attempt. The gorillas did not fail him, I did. Looking back, I wish I had helped him by encouraging him to simply hang out with us and the gorillas.

Lots of people treated it as a game and larked around but others were genuinely inquisitive. The thing about the gorillas was that the more you wondered about them, the more there was to wonder about. Out looking for volunteers, I came across a middle-aged man and his father. Dressed in almost identical anoraks, they were central European and had a dignified comportment. The father did not speak English; his son translated my request, which they quietly discussed. They were happy to oblige and followed me to the gorillas. Other people made way for them as they took their place in front of the camera.

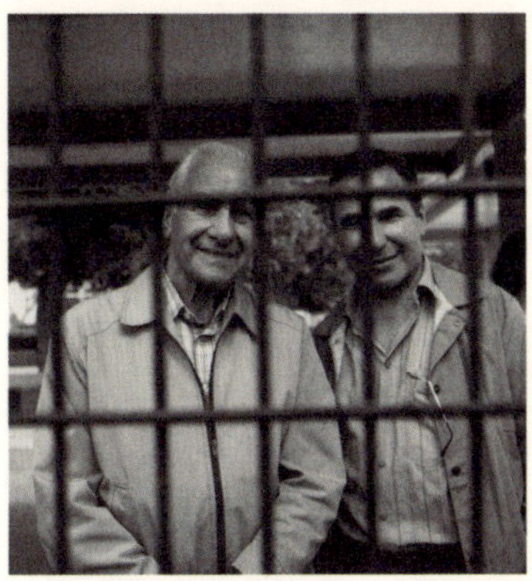

One of Salome's photographs

And there they stood, benign smiles on their faces, patiently waiting as they respectfully addressed themselves to the gorilla and the camera. I do not think I have ever seen anything as noble or wise, for making a portrait takes place on both sides of the camera, as the big hairy hand and sad amber eyes brought home.

The ballad of Mike Disfarmer features such an extraordinary character, the lyrics flirt with fiction. As it was, Disfarmer invented himself, along with his name. He was born Mike Meyer in Indiana in either 1882 or 1884. The son of German immigrants, his father had fought for the North in the Civil War, and afterwards moved to the South, where he became a rice farmer. In 1914, eight years after his father's death, the family settled in Heber Springs, a spa town with a then-thriving tourist scene. In partnership with a photographer called Penrose, Meyer set up a portrait studio in the lobby of the Jackson Hotel, where folk in their finest could have their portrait taken in front of a *trompe-l'oeil* backdrop before going into the theatre. When the hotel burned down in 1921, Penrose left town, leaving Meyer on his own. Over the next few years, he bought some land just off Main Street and built a studio with a fifteen-foot tall, north-sloping window. On Thanksgiving Day 1926, a tornado tore through Heber Springs, flattening the family home. With nowhere else to go, Meyer moved into his studio, and lived there alone for the rest of his life until he was found dead on the floor, nibbled by rats, in 1959.

A self-portrait from 1950 shows a gaunt figure with pursed lips in a tall, black Homburg and heavy-rimmed glasses. With his face three-quarters to the camera, he's looking straight through the lens with the eyes of someone conscious that the lens is looking straight through him. Mike Meyer had an uncompromising sense of self. In 1939, five years after his mother's death, as the incredulous townsfolk read in the *Heber Springs Times*, Meyer had his name legally changed to Disfarmer. He had never been a Meyer, he explained, but had been blown into the Meyer family by a tornado when he was three years old. In his understanding, Meyer (or Meier) was German for a farmer, and he wanted to shed this old name to distance himself from what he believed was a misleading identity. Not the shrewdest move from a local businessman whose clients were predominantly farmers, but typical of Disfarmer. In a God-fearing community of Baptists, he openly rejected the Bible and drank beer for breakfast. Tall and dishevelled, he wore a long black coat, never married and reputedly had only one friend. Children were afraid of him; they used to hide outside his studio, and when he appeared, they would run off screaming. Trying to explain what he was like, Bessie Uttley, his former assistant, said: 'Mr. Disfarmer was a person that nobody would never understand if they lived to be a million years old. You know, he would make fun of the people that would come in there. He didn't exactly make fun of them, but it was like he had a brain and like we never had . . . by acting like he did, it made the people kind of think he was nutty, which I knew he wasn't. They were afraid of him, yet they'd go there by the dozens.'

His portrait studio was the only show in town, or as Bessie put it: 'Mike had the world by the tail, and it was a downhill pull because he didn't have no competition . . . They'd line up just like it was a bargain basement and, on Saturdays, boy, I'll tell you that was something. Them gals out in the country, they deliberately loved to have their pictures made. If they'd go to town and have their pictures made one week, they were just as likely to go to town and have it made the next. It was a fad, kind of, to go and have a hamburger and have a picture made. The only time that Mike would suffer would be when these carnivals would come through, and they'd make little photographs – real quick photographs. 'Course, they weren't as good as Mike's.'

Lacking the glamour of the Jackson Hotel's lobby, Disfarmer's new place was more photographer's studio rather than portrait salon. It had blank walls with a choice of either a black curtain or a backdrop of white panels stuck in place with black tape. The only props were a couple of wooden tables and a bench. Technically, the studio's soft light from a huge skylight was ideal; aesthetically, the surroundings were more of an interrogation chamber. Disfarmer placed practicalities ahead of pleasantries and was seemingly blind to social mores. It was said that he used to bang a cowbell to command eye contact from his clients. Formally, the stark backdrop and the flood of overhead light entomb Disfarmer's subjects in a blank box, their sun-baked features stilled into sculptures. The desolate minimalism maroons them, their veins filling with formaldehyde as they awaited his instructions. 'As children, we were afraid of him,' said Tom Olmstead, a Heber Springs funeral director who was photographed by Disfarmer as a child. 'He looked that bad, he was scary.' Micky Barnett, a local doctor and historian, dismissed Disfarmer as a 'weirdo'. 'He had such a slow shutter speed, he had to explain to his subject: "Now listen you all gotta be still." People have said he would actually tell us not to blink . . . Now we've got somebody, one, trying not to move, two, trying not to blink their eyes when they feel like they need to, and that to me is an uncomfortable situation. And what I see when I look at the picture, is he has saturated the person with thoughts, and they're standing there trying to obey all the rules he's laid down before he takes the picture. I'm told he would have a genius for capturing the person at their natural best, and what I see in them is not at all what they were like when I was standing talking to them on the street.'

Embalmed under Disfarmer's skylight, his subjects face us from his netherworld. Motionless, mouths closed, eyes wide open, they submit to his camera's pitiless gaze. Normally, such a stare is taboo, a fleeting glance being the way of the world, but in the hands of this crank, there are no nuances. In his long black coat, Disfarmer tramples personal space and eyeballs his subjects, banging his cowbell. Although the majority of his clients were young people out on the town, the quintessential Disfarmer portrait prized in books and exhibitions shows hard lives and calloused faces, not youth and Saturday smiles. The trademark setting accentuates their austerity; people materialise like ghosts in loose suits and workwear.

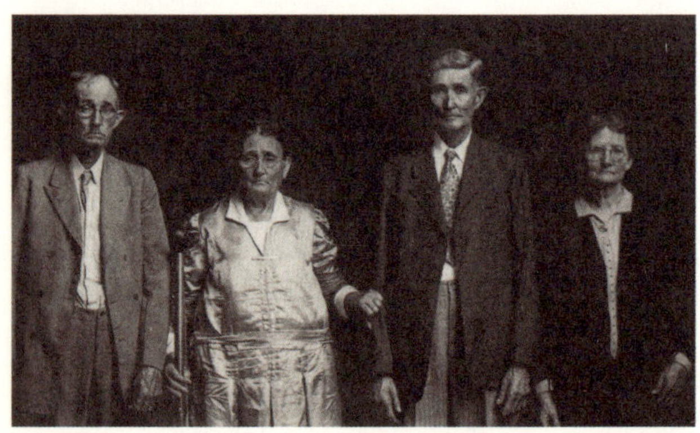

Mike Disfarmer, *c.*1930

In an unidentified portrait circa 1930, the four elderly subjects, two men and two women, stand before a fathomless black background, into which they are in danger of receding without trace. The woman in a satin dress holds a crutch and grasps a man's sleeve. The men wear mismatching jackets and trousers. One has his tie tucked into his shirt, the other is so thin the arms of his jacket hang in loose folds, and the veins in their hands protrude like old wiring. Crumpled figures pictured in the gloaming of their lives, their gaunt faces stare out from across the Styx.

There are echoes of Grant Wood's *American Gothic* (1930) in the ideologically satisfying mythology of these Heber Springs farmers. Gnarled survivors of tornadoes and the Great Depression, cyphers for God Bless America's stoical self-sufficiency, Disfarmer's weather-beaten folk appear onstage at a safe distance from the affluent North. Misplaced parallels have been drawn between Disfarmer's dungarees and the dark-robed portraits of the renowned German photographer August Sander's Westerwald farmers. Justly celebrated for the understated diction of his photography, Sander's maxim 'no unexplained shadows' became a byword for an aesthetic that honoured clarity and understatement over expressionism and exaggeration. Sander's over-arching project, 'Citizens of the Twentieth Century', sought to create a typology of German society; an Icarian task, for unlike actors, individuals cannot be typecast. Nonetheless, Sander's dignified photography exemplified a respectful approach to portraiture and attained its zenith in his pictures from the Westerwald. In their dark suits and wing collars, securely grounded in their identity as *Bauernfamilie*, Sander's farmers meet his lens on equal terms, an understanding and a respect absent in Disfarmer's *modus operandi*.

More akin to Disfarmer's dystopian drama are Richard Avedon's notorious 'In the American West' photographs; portraits of the 'men and women who work at hard uncelebrated jobs, the people who are often ignored and overlooked'. A laudable enterprise, possibly, but one whose sincerity would be sorely compromised in the hands of this fashion photographer. A reference photograph from 1979 shows Jimmy Lopez, a gypsum miner in Sweetwater, Texas, posing for the camera. On the blazing hot June day, flanked by three assistants, Avedon placed Jimmy in front of a white backdrop attached to a workshop's exterior wall. Standing in the shade cast by the plant's tall building, Jimmy faces the dazzling sunshine bouncing back off the wall opposite, his eyes tightly closed against the glare, his face caked white with gypsum. Avedon then manipulated the negative to maximise its contrast and produced a picture measuring 56 x 45 inches. A spectacular piece of showmanship, the print's starkness and scale transform Jimmy into a graphically arresting extra from Central Casting. A bug on a pinboard would be an apt analogy.

All too predictably, 'In the American West' proved a roaring success. The Amon Carter Museum had commissioned Richard Avedon, in return for which they received a full set of the 124 photographs, an investment whose value rapidly surpassed the museum's original outlay. When the show toured to the ICA in Boston, attendance leapt from their usual five thousand to a record twenty-seven thousand. The Amon Carter Museum invited many of the 'overlooked' to the grand opening, a cohort notably absent from the museum's usual guest list. They subsequently attended a public discussion at the museum, where several went on record to state that they felt honoured, not exploited, by Avedon's portraiture. According to Irvin Lippman, a director of the museum, one of them, a trucker called Billy Mudd, 'saw his photograph in the museum and said that he has been literally looking for himself for years, and finally found himself in the museum . . . that he had finally felt that God was speaking through his eyes'.

By the end of the fifties, the sixty-five-year-old Disfarmer was subsisting on chocolate ice-cream. When he had not appeared at the grocery store for a while, some neighbours forced open the studio door and found his corpse lying on newspaper. He was buried without a headstone. When the bank cleared the derelict studio, among the obsolete equipment they discovered boxes containing four thousand glass negatives, which were bought for the token sum of $5 by Joe Allbright, a former mayor of Heber Springs. No value was placed on the mouldy archive of this odd photographer who had charged fifty cents for a portrait session, but Joe Allbright regarded Disfarmer's photography as a part of the town's history. He gave the negatives to Peter Miller, the editor of the local newspaper, and each week *The Sun-Times* published one of Disfarmer's portraits and invited readers to write in for a free print if they were in the picture. Miller had a good knowledge of photography and believed Disfarmer's portraits deserved a wider audience, so he sent a few examples to *Modern Photography* magazine. Julia Scully, the editor, was impressed: 'They were so powerful, so immediate.' Wanting to know more, she went down to Heber Springs to meet Miller and learn about Disfarmer. Realising that there would be examples of his portraits in general circulation, she started buying them in local thrift stores and compared these to the ones Miller had been given. Together, they resolved to produce a book of the portraits.

Their book, *Disfarmer: Heber Springs Portraits, 1939–1946; From the Collections of Peter Miller and Julia Scully* (1976), was accompanied by an exhibition at New York's International Center of Photography, posthumously elevating the small-town misfit to photography's pantheon. The resurrection of Disfarmer's small, technically imperfect, prints into handsomely framed enlargements on hallowed white walls, transformed them into archetypes of resilient homesteaders. Heber Springs family names were now fine art titles and Disfarmer's unvarnished aesthetic was being waxed lyrically. All the newly printed portraits were produced from the salvaged cache of glass negatives, which dated from the period 1939–46, and constituted barely ten percent of his entire work. By selecting examples attuned to their taste, Peter Miller, Julia

Scully and the other curators distilled Disfarmer's work into a distinctly coherent body purporting to be truly representative of his aesthetic. Whether their curation coincided with the photographer's ambitions can never be substantiated, for Disfarmer left no records or interviews elucidating his agenda. Dead and gone, Disfarmer's silence suited the *cognoscenti*, granting them free licence to define his aesthetic and cast him as photography's gothic weirdo.

In 2004 Michael Mattis, a prominent photography collector, was contacted by a young couple from Heber Springs who had accumulated fifty original Disfarmer portraits from their extended family's albums and picture frames. Mattis saw an opportunity, seized it and bought the lot for $20,000. Vintage prints are the holy grail of photography, and the provenance of these, straight from the subjects' palms, set the gold standard. Mattis chose a young, amiable art researcher, Hava Gurevich, as 'the perfect person to insert herself in a quiet way into the local community of picture finders'. Masterminded from Mattis' turreted mansion in Scarsdale (the wealthiest town on America's East Coast), they recruited locals from Heber Springs to track down as many original Disfarmers as possible. Mattis is shown in a photograph standing in front of a limousine holding a sheaf of Disfarmers, flanked by a pair of his scouts. 'We put a big war map on their wall and set out to go down every dirt road within a fifty-mile radius of Disfarmer's studio.' Mattis instructed the recruits to prioritise portraits of adults over children, dungarees over dress suits and trained them to compile 'Sotheby's- or Christie's- level condition reports'. Driving around with little photo-scanners, they paid the families between fifty and a few hundred dollars per portrait, leaving behind a replacement facsimile print; Mattis would pay his collaborators up to two thousand dollars for the original.

Word spread fast. Heber Springs was, and remains, an impoverished community and the lure of an unexpected windfall created what Ellen Hobgood, the owner of a neighbourhood art gallery and painting workshop, called 'a feeding frenzy' There were dark tales of relatives rifling through family albums. As Dr Micky Barnett, from the Cleburne County Historical Society, observed: 'They changed from pictures of my grandmother to money.' Steven Kasher, a New York photography dealer, caught wind of this enterprise and made a deal with two of Mattis' agents, Rhonda and Jamie Heaver, who later claimed to have earned several hundred thousand dollars ferreting out Disfarmers. In the end, Mattis' campaign yielded over three thousand photographs and he subsequently sold hundreds through the Edwynn Houk gallery in New York for between $7,500– $24,000 each.

Author of his own history, Mattis described his role as 'educating an initially sceptical rural community' about Disfarmer's 'objects of significant artistic and cultural value' and saw his actions as 'transferring wealth' to the poor Arkansans, albeit a tiny fraction of his multi-million-dollar profits. An ambitiously eminent patron of photography, Mattis's collection is famous and has been exhibited in museums such as the Barnes Foundation, Philadelphia. Interviewed for a documentary about Disfarmer, revealingly, he is pictured in his study with the Diane Arbus photograph *Boy with a straw hat waiting to march in a pro-war parade, N.Y.C.*, 1967, on the wall behind him. He might as well have had a hunting rifle by his side and a tiger's head on the wall. Caught in the glare of Diane Arbus's flash like a suspect at a crime scene, the pimply-faced young man with big ears and an incongruous boater faces her lens with the same naïve obedience as Disfarmer's subjects. An American flag at his side, a huge GOD BLESS AMERICA SUPPORT OUR BOYS badge on one lapel, a BOMB HANOI on the other, the boy lines up before Arbus like a lamb for the slaughter, a volunteer for her *a priori* portrait of cynically malign melodrama. Minted in the silver second of her exposure, his righteous certainty and wide-eyed gaze proclaim brittle conviction in a shrill voice. Cast into popular culture as the epitome of the hideous contradictions straddling idealism and extremism, patriotism and militarisation, the youth is condemned in the flare of the camera's *auto-da-fé*, the dark street behind him his comfortless grave. Had he known he was about to be burned alive in an iconic photograph, he might not have so readily acted the part of an obligingly grotesque idiot, but dazzled by her attention, he stood blind in the photographer's theatre, his portrait delivered with the aplomb of a punchline. Live on the night, the stalls rocked with laughter, but as the years and decades pass, and the geology of the ambiguities settles, the heat of the moment is fossilised in a cold light. History is ill-served by crass polemic; compassion illuminates understanding, exposing within the harsh contrasts of black and white a fuller spectrum of tones.

But the photograph never exits stage left. The exclamation hangs in the air. The *Boy with a straw hat waiting to march in a pro-war parade, N.Y.C., 1967*, stares back, his face the spectre of a victim shaming the world's contempt. This young man was never a fictional character, his portrait never a film still; that was him on that day, condemned in the merciless tones of an ambitious prosecutor. Defenceless, this cruel depiction enters the record. Such a photograph admits no caveat; the charge stands as read. In Disfarmer's studio his subjects stand similarly in the dock, surrendering their identities to the photographer's process. Recontextualised from Heber Springs to a collector's wall, their injustice is assimilated into a trophy. One such collector, Carl Sander, has a portrait of a woman in a gingham dress holding her toddler child, who stands beside her on the corner of a low table or stool. On the back of the vintage print, the woman has written: '. . . is no good, he took it before I knew it. Was looking at mom. Tear it up if you want to, Charles was scared.'

To Carl Sander, 'Disfarmer wasn't really interested in taking intimate portraits. He was interested, I think, in realising his own vision of what he wanted the photograph to be like, and I think that the people in the community, their role, in respect to Mike Disfarmer . . . they allowed themselves to be manipulated. I mean it's one thing to say, he caught me off guard once, but it's another to say then I sent my mother and my father and my kids and I went back every year. I think that there was some fascination with this very oddball character and there was some fascination, conscious or unconscious, with playing their role in whatever that theatre was.' Absent in this analysis is any reflection by the collector on the role he is playing and the values he is espousing. His prism serves his own purposes, patronising the Heber Springs subjects with his convenient conclusions.

Casting the woman and her son as mere players fictionalises their existence, just as the camera can insulate the photographer from actual human interaction, a shield separating them from social and moral norms, abstracting a living presence into an optical projection. In portraiture, photography's sustained engagement allows the possibility of seeing past the casting and into the character, its silent stare creating a space into which the person can emerge as themselves. Disfarmer's indifference bordered on antipathy, a disinterest which could register as insensitivity. His studio, blank walls shaped around the skylight with little, if any consideration, for ambience, prioritised technical criteria over consideration for the clientele's comfort or ease. Not surprisingly, uncertainty filled the silence. Some believe that Disfarmer's intimidatory atmosphere was penetrating. 'The pictures are psychological bullets,' opines Michael Mattis, 'they go through the people and really capture what they're all about.' This attitude embodies the smoking gun of photography's pirates. A philosophical divide separates those who conceive photography to be the reception of the image of the light's traces distinct from those who imagine that they are shooting an image. The predominant trace on a 'shot' photograph is cordite.

The most mysterious aspect of Disfarmer's life lay on the other side of the camera, his subjects. When Julia Scully attempted to research Disfarmer's history, she found that little was known about him, a puzzling factor given the small-town character of Heber Springs; people's testimonies proved disparate and contradictory. All the surviving subjects who could provide first-hand accounts were very young when they were photographed, and Disfarmer's treatment of children was notoriously inconsiderate. It was only when the lid to his life was prised open by the publishers and curators, and he was prominently reframed in photography's forum, that the Disfarmer folklore mushroomed. Quotidian accounts and banal portraits did not whet the appetite of the metropolitan vanguard hungry for eerie anecdotes of this 'Zorro-like figure'. Twilight tales from a shadowy history conjured a black-robed Mephistopheles in the studio off Main Street; hardly the persona of a small-town portrait photographer, cranky or otherwise, who had previously been taken for granted. Possibly people accepted Disfarmer's portraits uncritically, resigned to an absence of choice; a bad barber is better than none at all.

A portrait from the mid-1930s features two sisters in their early twenties. One is blind. She stands on the right wearing dark glasses, leaning slightly forwards in what might be her usual posture. She and her sister wear pretty dresses, and their hair is set in beautiful waves. Positioned side on to the camera, they are turned to face the lens. The sighted sister is holding an alligator handbag. Behind her dark glasses, the blind sister has an impassive look on her face. Her sister's stance is more active; her feet are splayed, and she meets the lens with a searching, almost protective gaze, unsure of its motives or testimony.

Some would argue that Disfarmer's portraits should be valued for their sociological value, that his lifetime's work created a record of this insular farming community. But the problem with some records is that in the absence of other material, the sole account becomes the official account, taken at face value, unquestioned by contradictory voices. And photographic portraiture is the most subjective of records. A near contemporary of Disfarmer was the Swedish photographer John Alinder, who also photographed a rural society. Like Disfarmer, Alinder turned his back on farming. He was born in Sävasta, Uppland, in 1878, a prosperous agricultural community about fifty miles north of Stockholm. Alinder was left a farm in a will, but, in an ironic parallel with Disfarmer, rejected the idea of being a farmer and declined it, an unheard-of response which was viewed as a scandal. A self-portrait in his mid-thirties shows a handsome man with big ears, a moustache and a smile standing beside his garden fence. A summer's day, the light streams through the leaves of the trees behind him as he poses barefoot on the grass. He looks at ease with the camera and with life. Alinder lived in Sävasta all his life, aptly described with wry Nordic understatement as a rebel who stayed at home. He devoted himself to portrait photography, a career he helped sustain by running a general store (and sometime speakeasy) from his home.

Unlike Disfarmer's macabre studio setting, Alinder's portraits are at large in the community. Photographed outside in the summer, occasional camera-fright aside, people are relaxed in their *Wild Strawberries* surroundings. Sitting on a bench in the garden, holding a cat in the shade of a tree, or seated in a bough, Alinder's compositions embrace the setting; the place is as much a feature of the community as the people themselves. Collectively, all these portraits form Alinder's depiction of rural domesticity. Often, photography monographs of portraiture contain too many pictures, the weaker examples deafening the clarity of the art. In Alinder's case, the opposite is true; certainly, some portraits have more presence than others, but cumulatively they form a choir. All these voices, all bound together by their relationship to the place, they each appear at home, and together their portraits create a hymn to their homeland. The distinctiveness of the time and place and people make it seem as if they are all part of a film. From the static realism of the photograph, it is as though they could step out into moving celluloid and emerge into that summer of their lives.

The summer vision of early twentieth-century Uppland looks idyllic: the wooden houses are homely, the trees have thick foliage, and the grass is ankle-deep. Apart from their attire, the only nod to modernity are the steel bicycles some men hold by their side. The people's faces are round and healthy; none are as gaunt as the Arkansas farmers. Life was evidently much harder in Heber Springs, although the rationale guiding the recent reappraisal of Alinder's portraits was the polar opposite of the gothic agenda that shaped Disfarmer's legacy. Published to accompany an exhibition at *Landskrona Foto* in 2021, the organisers sifted through 8,421 glass negatives that were rediscovered in the basement of a local library. Not one of the portraits in their selection would make their subjects or families baulk, let alone wince. Nor would they bring glee to the eyes in an auction. There is nothing edgy or disturbing about them: they are mercifully free of double exclamation marks or cheap thrills. Instead of Disfarmer's pitiless compositions, Alinder's have a kind-hearted friendliness, an attribute honoured by the curators.

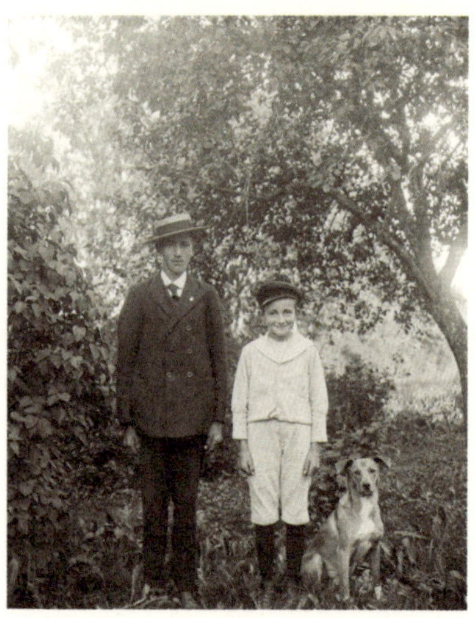

John Alinder, *c.*1910–20

The twinkle in the eye of his self-portrait is there in his portraits of fellow Upplanders. Self-taught, Alinder was unencumbered by superficial values. His portraits have the emotional warmth of family snaps, framed within handsome compositions. Far from being characteristic of the *ingenu*, this intuitiveness taps into the absolute wisdom of portrait photography; at its very best, it is a meeting of minds, of hearts. His large format, tripod-mounted camera is like an apple pie: a thing of goodness that they are going to share. People bring their pets. A man, his son, and their dog pose for the camera; all in a line, the father solemn, the boy beaming, the dog with his eye on something. A plum tree arches behind them, filtering the lowing sun. A girl in a striped dress holds her tabby cat, its long tail hanging down below her arm; an elderly lady sits in an ornate chair with an owl on her hand; a young man in jacket and waistcoat and cap holds a little bird in his cupped palm, his face flushed with delight. Some say that those who are now dead are alive in the photographs, but immediately the shutter closes, that verb reverts to the past tense. Photography is the look that Orpheus stole; it cannot keep that breath alive. Photography is instant retrospection. As bittersweet as an old letter, as evocative as a scent from childhood, its threads unravel eidetic memories from the basements of our minds. Agnes Johansson poses in her gingham dress with her short brown hair neatly brushed. The light is as soft as breath. She stands beside a gnarled old tree, its black, peeling bark sculpted in the silver of the glass negative. Beside it, Agnes is almost ethereal. Gently, she holds the palm of her left hand against the trunk, almost as one might place a hand on a dog's head. Her face is impassive as she looks directly into the lens, directly into her photograph.

*

Seydou Keïta, the Malian photographer, was born in Bamako in 1921. His father was a carpenter, but Keïta's apprenticeship was side-tracked by an uncle who gave him a camera. Smitten, the fourteen-year-old taught himself the basics and started photographing his friends and family. For the next decade or so, Seydou Keïta supplemented his growing portraiture business by working for his family, until in 1948 his father gave him a little house behind the city's main prison which he turned into a studio. Despite its chilling location ('a place where no one wanted to live') Keïta's studio benefited from being close to the centre of town, unlike the city's other photographers who were based further away. Keïta's disarmingly simple philosophy would have been an anathema to Disfarmer: 'When you're a photographer, you always have to come up with ideas to please the customer. My experience taught me the positions that my customers liked best. You try to obtain the best pose, the most advantageous profile, because photography is an art, everything should be as close to perfection as possible. After all, the customer is only trying to look as good as possible. In Bamako we say *i ka nyè tan*, which in English means "you look well", but in fact it means "you look beautiful like that". Art is beauty.'

Initially, Keïta used a fringed bedspread as a backdrop; subsequently, he would change the fabric every few years. (He could date a portrait by its backdrop.) Some of his clients wore the traditional *boubou*, its voluminous shape cool in the heat, but others, particularly the younger men who formed most of his customers, wanted to be photographed in European suits. Catering to the theatricality of the event, Keïta acquired a range of clothing and accessories: different styles of suits and shirts, kipper ties and hats; watches, fountain pens and handkerchiefs; plastic flowers, telephones, radios and clocks; bicycles and scooters and, eventually, four cars (a Peugeot, a Dauphine, a Versailles and a Sylla, an American model). An early portrait shows a little boy in a pair of shorts, braces holding them up over a striped shirt, his *petit français* costume topped by an oversized beret. He has one hand in his pocket and the other holds the handlebars of a shiny bicycle with thick tyres. Scraps of litter on the earthen floor undermine the aspirational props, as do the sores and dust on the little boy's legs. Even so this is his day, and he looks out towards the photographer, watching with a child's tentative curiosity, an innocent response to the portrait session that Keïta honours. At the metaphysical heart of his portraits is empathy.

Seydou Keïta frequently posed his clients so that they were facing diagonally out of the picture, an oblique dynamic adding verve and depth to the composition. By facing towards the brightest side of the studio, the person's dark skin would be bathed in light, the pose of their faraway look uninhibited by the lens. 'The angle portrait was my invention. I had positioned a woman like that and I thought she was really attrac-

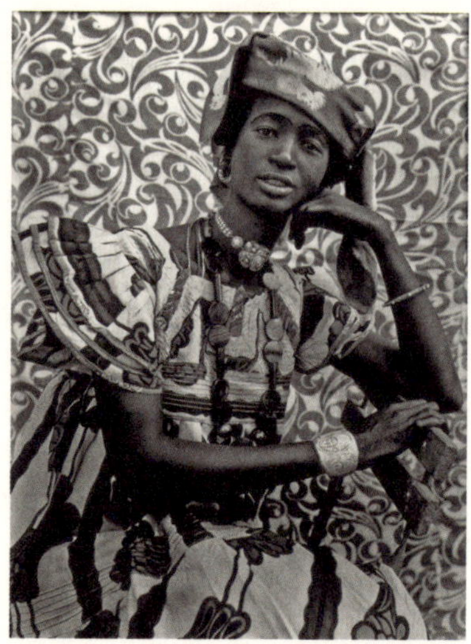

Seydou Keïta, untitled and undated

tive, she also liked it.' A technically accomplished photographer, Keïta's handsome portraits are formed from sharp focus and ample depth of field. In costume, his clients attain a glimpse of fantasy beyond their everyday. A portrait from their imaginations, the studio's backdrop set the stage for their theatre. Keïta saw his role as being in the service of their portrait; rather than bit parts serving his agenda, they were singing their own songs.

Some of the portraits soar from the quotidian to the empyrean through the dance of the kaleidoscopic patterns of the women's batik outfits against the decoration of Këïta's backdrops. 'Sometimes the background went well with their clothes,' he recalled, 'but it was all haphazard.' Emblazoned in the graphic tones of his black-and-white photography, the petals and flowers on a woman's flamboyant dress sing out over the *fleur-de-lys* curls of the backdrop, her cockerel-embroidered headscarf triumphantly crowning her pencilled eyebrows. Another lady beams out from under her wax-print headscarf and dress, the chequered backdrop adding a jamboree of contrasts. Magnificently unpredictable, like a comet tearing through the staid conventions of Western portraiture, these riotous portraits blaze a trail of cultural independence in a carnival of two-tone.

Some self-portraits perform to a make-believe audience; a chance to create a look when no one is looking. The Nigerian photographer, Samuel Fosso, was born partially paralysed. His grandfather, an Igbo healer, gradually nursed him back to health, but the Biafran War forced Fosso to flee his home, and eventually he settled with an uncle in Bangui, in the Central African Republic. He began taking photographs when he was ten, and in 1975, aged only thirteen, he took over an empty portrait studio. With limited equipment, he had to process his rolls of film overnight at another studio and would use up any spare frames by doing self-portraits. At first, he wanted to send them to his grandmother who had raised him back in Nigeria. 'Sometimes when I made photographs that I was not satisfied with, where I didn't feel beautiful inside, I would cut up the negatives instead of printing them.

But if I felt that the image was beautiful or represented how I felt inside, then I would print the image and keep the negative.'

The Central African Republic of the 1970s was a repressive autocracy; even bell bottoms and platform boots were banned. As an Igbo, masquerade and body art were part of Fosso's heritage, and as a teenager, he loved 'Highlife' music and danced to Prince Nico Mbarga's *Sweet Mother*. Behind closed doors, in the privacy of his self-portraits, Fosso was free to explore his own sense of self, his own ideas of what it felt to be beautiful. Framed by the dishes of his studio's lights, dressed in high-waisted black bell bottoms, a white shirt with huge lapels, sleeves rolled up, a chunky gold watch dangling from his wrist, in a Kodak cap and sunglasses, Fosso looks over to his left, an insouciant figure posing on a chequered floor with batik backcloth. The light hits the frames of his glasses and bounces off the backs of the studio lights, illuminating the whole scenario as a *mise-en-scène*. Playing on the idea of the self-portrait as a portrait of a self-portrait, Fosso photographs himself peeking out from between two batik backdrops, the textiles transformed into theatre curtains, as his partially visible figure looks away from the camera, absorbed in the act of his own drama.

In 1994, Fosso was invited to exhibit his work at the Rencontres de Bamako, a festival of photography organised by Mali's Ministry of Culture and the Institut Français. Encouraged by the response to his pictures, Fosso granted himself a new licence for his *métier*. 'I first realised that I was an artist when I found out that my main task was to create. I then said to myself that if what I had been doing as a job was art, why not continue regardless of whether I had clients or not?' This placed him in a financial dilemma, but when the French department store Magasins Tati commissioned him, along with the Malian photographers Seydou Keïta and Malick Sidibé, to work on a project in Paris, he realised he could use the opportunity to his advantage. Magasins Tati envisioned that the three West African photographers would produce pictures based on their black-and-white style, but Fosso confounded these expectations by working in colour. 'Since there were three African photographers, I wanted my project to register a different mood of the African imagination, and not the images that were already associated with African photography.'

Clad in leopard skins on a leopard skin throne, wearing Asante gold and the silver *manilla*, the slave-traders' bracelet, Fosso presents himself as *The Chief: He who Sold Africa to the Colonists*, (1997), a panto-mime Mobutu Sese Soko figure mocking Metropolitan France's idea of Africa. The stage is splendidly cynical; a cacophony of printed textiles in vivid colours layer the floor and wall, satirising the tradition in West African studio portraiture. Placed at his feet are a pair of snazzy shoes and a leather bag, spoofing the European delight in ridiculing product placement. As a finishing touch, His Highness, in ivory sunglasses and a fur hat, holds four tall sunflowers and adopts a cod regal pose. A cartoon of colonially inspired consumerism, his technicolour lampoon has the last laugh, mocking the knowingness implicit in the metropolis's patronising cultural appreciation.

Samuel Fosso stuck his finger in this portraiture's unhealed wound. Although Seydou Këita's two-tone settings pop the velvet-curtained pomposity of salon portraiture, there is a blood-stained trail leading back to the black-and-white Lamprey grids used by nineteenth-century Western anthropologists, backdrops as demeaning as the height marking in police mugshots. Among the elites, a figure holding a high-status object is cast as an elite, an affectation patronisingly regarded as aspirational when transposed to those without power. Sandro Botticelli's and Hans Memling's young men holding a medallion and a Roman coin respectively (1470s–1480s) portray figures of indisputable social rank, while a West African holding a transistor radio might elicit sniggers from some Western viewers. Fosso refused to comply with this history, and staged his own theatre for his own ends. As did Muddy Waters. In 1941, when Muddy Waters was still working on a Mississippi plantation, Alan Lomax recorded him for the Library of Congress. Afterwards, Muddy Waters took his 78 rmp record to a Black portrait studio. Wearing a beautiful double-breasted suit with a kipper tie and gleaming leather shoes, holding the record in his left hand, he sits for the portrait with an artist's quiet pride, refusing to acquiesce to the subordinate status imposed on him.

In an adroit subversion of this tradition, the photographer Silvia Rosi (b. 1992) enacted a series of portraits depicting her Togolese parents, who had emigrated to Italy from West Africa. In *Self-portrait as my father, 2020,* photographed against a blue backdrop, she sits on a pink pedestal wearing spectacles, a blazer and tie, with a pile of books balanced on her head. In her left hand, and spread around the floor in neat little piles, are big red tomatoes. In an interview discussing her work and the context of West African studio portraiture, Rosi refers to the dignity and pride of this tradition. 'Social class does not matter, everyone has the opportunity to display a better version of themselves and that's what I like the most about those photographs. But the reality is different, there are more complex dynamics, so in my work I perform in the opposite way. I show the ugliest part of my family, the suffering and struggles that brought us here.'

Samuel Fosso's *The Chief: He who Sold Africa to the Colonists* exposes the heart of the problems surrounding vernacular studio portraiture; the disparity between the way it was seen by its original subjects, and its appraisal by a supposed elite. Removed and elevated from the place and purpose of its creation, it is perceived through a different prism. Supposedly unsophisticated responses are replaced by ones inflected with hubris. All too often knowingness is blindness. The very idea that taking a family portrait from Heber Springs to Scarsdale places it in the hands of a more perceptive viewer than the relative who could, and would, read far more into the nature of that familial likeness is preposterous. To overlook this fundamental bond that arises from photography, this Proustian quality of accessing layers of memory and the unconscious, is to lose focus on the very nature of photography itself. Remove introspection and all that remains is explanation. Art is not a problem to be solved, quite the reverse. Tapping into photography's fingerprint of the human existence initiates the beginning, rather than the conclusion, of the picture. The relationship between photographic memento and human memory need not be particular to the subject and the viewer, but without acknowledging this origin, its essence is stifled, and the photograph's subtleties go unwitnessed.

Peaceful Action: Photographic Memories of Anonymous Occupation Soldiers in Europe c.1946 (1990) is a book composed of portraits of American soldiers in Salzburg and Russian soldiers in Budapest, both sets taken as mementoes to send home. Posted abroad on active military service, these soldiers faced the very real prospect of going to war; they must have known that their portraits could possibly arrive posthumously. Culturally, the photographs are polarised. The

Russians' portraits are informed by an aesthetic from a previous century. They pose solemnly in front of a backdrop painted with a silver birch, or in gardens, or at a table decorated with flowers. Some of them brandish guns, standing to attention in their long coats and *ushankas,* but the hard façade of a faceless military is undone by the photography.

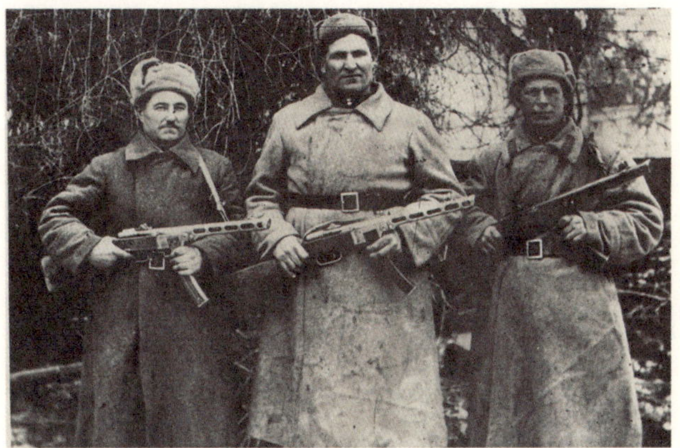

Photographer unknown. Russian soldiers, *c.*1946

Photography looks with a child's eye; it stares rudely and hasn't learned to overlook. Three male veterans of the Great Patriotic War stand in a line under a wintry tree. The biggest, a bear of a man, eyes shrouded under blunt features, looks at the camera inquisitively, the stock of his machine gun in his right hand, two fingers of his left hand curled around its magazine. The man on his right is smaller and older; he has a thin moustache and a serious countenance. To the left is a much younger man, his adolescent's face grown old, like the boy in Andrei Tarkovsky's *Ivan's Childhood*. In a series of portraits in front of the silver birch backdrop, soldiers pose revolver in hand, a playful but macabre amateur dramatic, some of them no more than boys. The older men with medals report to the camera with well-combed hair and polished boots. They could equally be groups of proud farmers. Occasionally there is a woman; in one, she wears a ribbon and a hair comb, and a medal on her chest.

Sitting on the front of their jeep, the Americans pose with Hollywood smiles, arms around their girlfriends. Two military police perform a Punch and Judy show, one with a truncheon, the other strumming a guitar. In another, behind a table piled with Coca-Cola, a corporal, more adolescent than young man, sits with his pal and their girls. Set in a dancehall or a club, outside the orbit of the camera's flash, figures move around in the background. One of the women wears her best smile, the other a level look; the men's smiles, whether wearing thin over the course of the night or through fear of imminent war, are as subdued as their military clothing. Unlike the Russian photographs, some of the Americans' negatives have become degraded over time, cracking the emulsion, forming black chasms in the photographs. A close-up of a GI raising a glass of beer, his face showered in flashlight, explodes into black ruptures, the emulsion unable to hold fast the evening's celebration, the party atmosphere consigned to damnation. Supposing there was a war and everyone went home.

Some of the American photographs have deteriorated so badly, the people's faces are obliterated. In others, the patina littering the negative smothers the image as though under fallen leaves, as opaque as a gravestone weathered beyond visibility. These blisters and scratches expose the vulnerability contained within the flesh of the original photograph. Beneath the emulsion's eczema, a man in a white shirt and tie sits with a little terrier on his knee. They are both looking away to their right, the man's attention, and the dog's, drawn to someone beyond the camera. The man holds the terrier gently in the crook of his arm, his left hand softly supporting the animal as it settles on his thigh. His right hand almost covers one of the terrier's front legs, his fingers resting on its paw. The terrier's right ear sits up, the left folds over. The flash has caught its nose and eyes, dabbing them with silver. Almost unscathed from the emulsion's craquelure, its face peers up at the unseen other, a look of trusting affection. The man's face is subsumed within the crazed glass of the wounded negative like a scratchy recording of his voice, but his words remain audible. Man and boy, he holds the warmth of his dog. From underneath the scars of time, the gentleness in his eyes is there to perceive, as the terrier's nose is about to twitch.

There are scarcely any examples of people posing

with their pets in Mike Disfarmer's portraits. Possibly they are quarantined beyond the editors' filters, excluded for being too ordinary or sentimental. Predictably, his most celebrated photograph featuring an animal shows a father and son standing behind a slaughtered stag. An exception is the portrait of Jarrett 'Pa' Hazelwood, *c.*1940–45, who is kneeling between his pair of bloodhounds. Working dogs, they have chains for leads and stare directly at the camera, their attention alerted; Jarrett is grinning, proud to be photographed with his hounds. This is their photograph, not Disfarmer's. It is doubly demanding to make a portrait of a person with their pet, for animals rarely keep still and often the person's attention is focused on calming the creature. Hardened hearts soften as their hands stroke the dog and the mask slips, showing a more vulnerable sense of self.

Libby Hall's *Prince and Others 1850–1940* (2000) is a pocket-sized book of *cartes de visite*, stereo and cabinet prints featuring portraits of dogs as well as dogs with their owners. Possibly promoted as a novelty book, and viewed accordingly by photography's canon, *Prince and Others* treads close to sentimentalism. But the sentimental is unearned emotion, and there is nothing saccharine or forced about the portraits in this book, surrounded as they are by portraits of dogs. Beauty and criteria are in the eye of the beholder. Portraits characterised by exclamation marks they are not; as nuanced exemplars of humanistic portraiture,

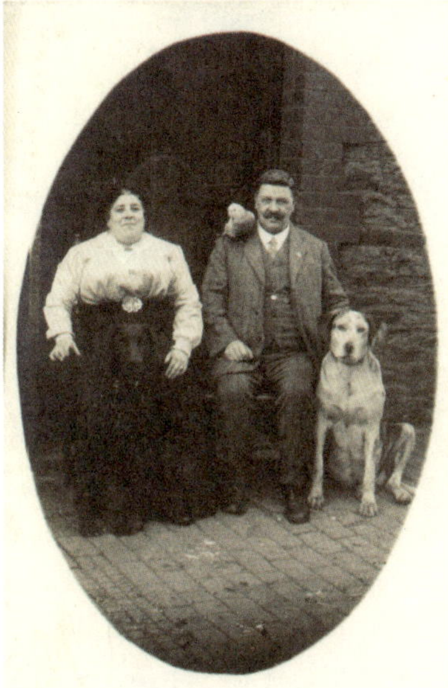

Photographer and date unknown

they excel. Emanating from an atmosphere of trust, gentleness, ease and unguardedness, the people with their pets display a presence rarely witnessed outside the privacy of the family. As studio portraits, they are the closest relative to amateur family photographs; portraits which, at their finest, are unparalleled in photographic portraiture. Framed within an oval composition, a middle-aged man in a moustache and three-piece suit, with a parrot on his shoulder, sits next to his wife, a jovial-faced matronly figure in a white blouse and long black skirt. They are seated outside some commercial premises, the building's stout wooden doors and brick and masonry walls foregrounded by stone-sett paving. A large, elderly white dog with dark ears sits at the man's side, his left hind leg splayed outwards, his old eyes peering at the photographer. The man rests his left hand on his dog's back and looks the camera in the eye. His wife, a twinkle in her eyes, looks slightly to the right of the camera, to where the photographer would have been standing beside the tripod. Almost hidden in the black shadows created by the folds of her dress, sits a black Labrador, nose and eyes also fixed on the photographer. Assembled in that oval for those minutes in which they prepared themselves for the camera, stepping aside from the day's routines, they composed themselves into an ensemble so honouring their quintet, it ventures into *verité*.

The raw privacy exposed in these portraits can be almost painful to behold. A late Victorian *carte de visite* shows a young man with a terrier sitting on his knee. Photographed in J. Rawlings' Paignton studio, the young man sits on an ornate velvet chair with tassels, the painted drape of a backdrop behind him. He wears a bowler hat and striped trousers. In contrast to his neat attire, the little dog is a scruffy creature. The terrier leans over to the right, its weight on one side. The man holds its other front leg in his left hand, and the dog's paw rests loosely on a fold in the man's trousers. The man's head is tilted to the right too, and like his dog, he leans on his right side. He is young and slightly effeminate with pale eyes and delicate features.

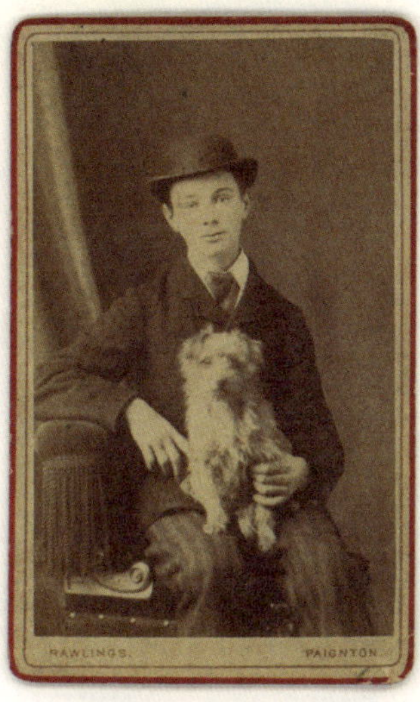

J. Rawlings, date unknown

His lips are slightly open, and the index finger of his right hand gently strokes the dog. The print is partially damaged by a crease, and there is a smudge over his right eye. The highlights are overexposed, so the skin on his face and the back of his right hand are an indistinct pale tone. The dog's head is ever so slightly blurred, just enough to soften its coat but sufficiently well-defined to show the line of its little mouth and the light in its sad eyes. Tenderly, the young man looks at the camera with the same wistful melancholy.

It would be wishing upon a star to expect to find multitudinous examples of introspectively profound portraits among the galaxy churned out by high street studios, not least because it is an almost impossible undertaking. Such a photographic portrait is, by definition, a publication of the most private expression – a person's sense of self. A truly insightful portrait, one whose presence is as trusting and open as that person would be in unguarded conversation, is more likely to arise where such a relationship already exists, which is why the most sensitive portraiture is generally to be found in the family album.

There is a place where this privacy is hidden in plain sight, behind a simple curtain. The once ubiquitous photobooth was invented by Anatol Josepho in 1925. The original 'Photomaton' charged twenty-five cents for a strip of eight photographs, which appeared at the then astonishing speed of eight minutes. It proved so popular, he sold it two years later for a million dollars. In the summer of 1968, an English art student called Dick Jewell started salvaging portraits from a photobooth on Brighton seafront. He would look on top and behind the machine; occasionally, he would find them lying on the ground, sometimes intact, sometimes ripped up. Later that year he moved to London and continued collecting them, concentrating on photobooths in Underground stations, and eventually he published a book. *Found Photos* (1978) is an annoyingly apt book. As humble as the booths, the five by six-inch book is bound with glue rather than stitching, and over time, the glue becomes brittle, making it impossible to open the book fully without loosening the pages. This forces the reader to peek between the pages, as though it were secretive or transgressive. With each reading, the spine cracks further, allowing more of the found photos to escape the clutches of publication.

There is nothing as lonely as an ID photo. It is the ultimate act of isolation in a disinterested world, stripping away from the individual any social bonds. Alone in a photobooth, a late middle-aged man responds to the machine's red light as he would to a figure of authority, anxious to fulfil the correct criteria, eyes fixed on the screen, his face a fingerprint for official purposes. The first frame caught him unawares, looking down at the mechanism, his furrowed countenance unwittingly exposed. Another man looks traumatised by the experience, his eyes wide with anxiety, his combover brushed wildly above his lined forehead. Dejected, the photograph was torn to pieces, which Dick Jewell reassembled into a mosaic. On the adjacent page, there are the torn remains of a larger picture of the man with a woman's hand above his head as she attempts to smooth his hair. Some bits of the photograph are missing, including the right-hand side of his face, leaving his left eye looking out from the edge of a void. Many of the photographs left behind, ripped up or thrown away, were simply an ill-timed blink, while others became angry wounds. A couple in their twenties, faces touching and eyes shining, fill the frame. Torn in four, one tear goes straight across the pupils of the girl's eyes. Another portrait, of a

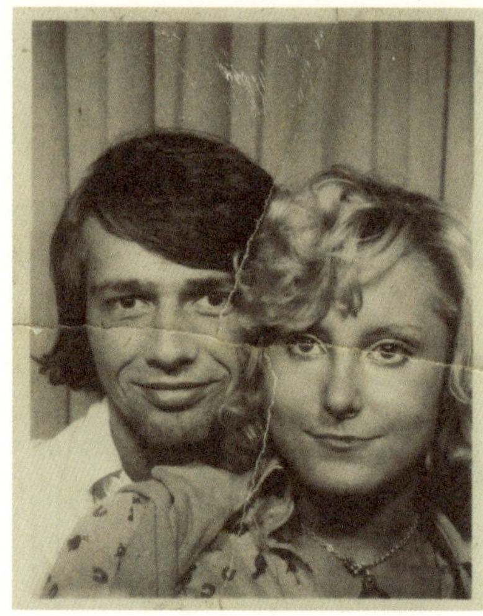

Photobooth photograph, date unknown

glamourous middle-aged woman in earrings and a scarf, has been torn into fifteen furious pieces.

While the portrait studio promises glamour, the photobooth is the great twenty-pence leveller. Sometimes, the booth's soulless confines drain all heart, the glum-faced defeated by the machine. For others, seemingly unselfconscious, an unfettered spirit shines out. A man in his sixties in glasses, a check jacket and tie, flashes a toothy smile. One of his shirt's lapels is sticking out over his jacket, and his head is slightly turned, leaving his ear protruding. A young woman in glasses poses like a nun in the first two frames; in the third, she opens her mouth as wide as a hippopotamus; in the last, she is blowing a raspberry. The photobooth was the kiosk-theatre, an auto portrait in four acts, its five seconds of fame flashing by as quickly as a kingfisher. A Woolworth's version of studio photography, you could be a star on a Saturday afternoon. A boy with long hair begins eyes front, and then turns his head, first one way, then the next, and grimaces for a finale. A man in a polo-neck jumper worn inside his shirt poses in a check jacket, his collar-length hair carefully brushed, eyes on the lens. This being the London Underground, not Hollywood, his hopeful brown eyes are tinged with doubt. The photobooth's lens set in its glass rectangle acts as a mirror; eyeing his reflection, he faces ahead, unsure how the picture of him on that afternoon might turn out.

– Photography's Realism –

The history of artists creating a realistic image in two dimensions from a fixed-point perspective is inseparable from the more technical history of optical drawing devices; the artist's eye was often viewing the composition through the engineer's invention. Albrecht Dürer made use of a drawing frame, as did John Constable three centuries later. The significance of the *camera obscura*, in particular, has been largely downplayed; a prejudicial blind spot occluding the history of art. The 'real image' in the *camera obscura* is not only a projection through a certain lens at a particular angle, but also a two-dimensional confirmation of the viewer's sense of realism. That Michelangelo Merisi da Caravaggio's paintings bore a corporeal realism, swelling beyond the confines of conventional flatness, owes much to his elaborate staging and use of the *camera obscura*, which provided composition, colour and light, from which he painted his 'assertive naturalism'. The 'film still' tableaux of contemporary photographic artists can be traced back to paintings such as Caravaggio's *The Supper at Emmaus* (c.1601). Amazed by Jesus' identity, St James's arms are outstretched, the fingers of his left hand almost reaching past the surface of the picture. The realism is accentuated by the finger-tips being ever so slightly soft – blurred? – possibly to convey the realism of the moment, or possibly a consequence of that detail in the *camera obscura* falling at the edge of focus, or maybe because Caravaggio's model simply could not keep his hand perfectly still. Alongside this gesture frozen mid-movement, Caravaggio paints the basket of fruit on the table with all the realism of their projection within the *camera obscura*. A still life surrounded by the swirl of life, Caravaggio places the basket so precariously on the edge of the table, the quotidian only adds to the tension.

Caravaggio not only used a *camera obscura* to cast an image of his *tableau vivant* in perspectival and chromatic accuracy, but also had a large *specchio a scudo* (a concave mirror) to reflect light, and even drilled a hole through his landlady's ceiling. His elaborate measures to create a perfectly lit and staged *mise en scène* remain secretive and concealed in the history of art. Beyond the pursuit of mimesis, the *camera obscura's* 'real image' served both as referent and polemic, casting a lantern slide of reality on the wall of Plato's cave. To regard the use of a *camera obscura* as akin to copying is facile, just as it is preposterous to claim that photography is purely a technique, as it blithely ignores not only the conception but the execution of the art.

A *camera obscura*, at its most literal and basic, is a darkened room with a pinhole in an exterior wall through which light passes, forming an inverted image on the interior wall opposite. Using a lens sharpens the image. Using two lenses, or a lens and a mirror, corrects the inversion. It not only displays this as a flat likeness with linear perspective, which can be copied or traced, it also reduces the tonal range to a smaller spectrum, creating a cohesive array of colour similar to the lantern aesthetic of projected film (as evident in Caravaggio's paintings). This 'real image' conjures an uncannily realism of the here and now, which would have been an almost necromantic effect in the pre-photographic world.

The fifth-century Chinese philosopher Mo Ti was the first to document the use of a form of *camera obscura*. In Western art, it was famously employed by Vermeer. His trademark setting of the room with the window on the left and the black-and-white floor has been proven to be a studio set complete with *camera obscura*. Research has revealed the location of the house (it's close to the train station) from which he painted *View of Delft* (1660–1663), a painting in all probability also created with the aid of a *camera obscura*. Arguably, Vermeer took his application of the *camera obscura* too far, as evidenced in his treatment of light, a characteristic of his paintings for which he is most respected, but which is ultimately unsatisfactory, for all the elegantly cool quotidian realism of his domestic scenes. When composing the image in the *camera obscura,* as the focus is pulled back from the foreground, the tiny spots of the brightest highlights lose their definition and become balls of light, termed 'circles of confusion'. Vermeer replicated this effect by depicting highlights as luminous globules, transposing the *camera obscura's* projection in paint. His celebrated treatment of light was undermined by his dogmatic, rather than deft, application of the *camera obscura.*

Human vision is a complicated series of observations and readjustments, scanning from the bright to the dark, making a series of readings to see more clearly. This is one reason why a photograph manifests greater contrast than an observation by the naked eye; there is only one reading, one exposure, which cannot register the entire spectrum. Similarly, the scene shown on a *camera obscura* is a fixed stare, unblinking between the spectrum's extremes. Unlike the eye, the single focus image is inflexible. The eye roams, the camera stares, absorbing everything passing through its lens.

The presence of the *camera obscura* in the history of art is confined to the shadows, a grudging acceptance that its monotone tracings were a template to be washed with colour or inked into a drawing. This limits its role to topographical drawings, ignoring aspects like colour and composition, and sees things in black and white. On a research visit to Oxford's History of Science Museum in 2016, I reassembled an early nineteenth-century *camera obscura* and focused it through the opened doors of their warehouse onto the scene outside. One by one the archivists looked at the image in the *camera obscura*, each one in turn, used to seeing exclusively monotone drawings from these devices, exclaimed: 'It's in colour!'

The *camera obscura* allowed artists to make intricate drawings with an apparently authentic sense of place and time of day (by including shadows etc.). For the military, its sharp-eyed accuracy made it ideal to record landscapes and encampments; in the nineteenth century, following Fox Talbot's invention, the British Army's Royal Engineers trained their surveyors to become the first generation of professional topographical photographers. Paul Sandby began his career as a military draughtsman, serving in the Board of Ordnance Drawing Room in Edinburgh before becoming the Duke of Cumberland's topographical artist on his Scottish campaigns. In 1765, Paul Sandby sketched and then painted a series of landscape studies of Luton Park, the Earl of Bute's newly acquired estate. Unlike the grand topographical views (such as Windsor Castle) for which he is well-known, these smaller scenes are more like nature studies; alive to the specifics of the place, perceived rather than conceived, convincingly naturalistic in incidental detail. Evoking a sense of place, of being in the then and there, they prefigure the *plein air études* of the late eighteenth and nineteenth centuries. Like an eyewitness account, their authenticity rests on the inclusion of seemingly insignificant details, the quotidian that history overlooks; an alert description, too banal to invent, quietly ringing with truth.

Reflecting its more prosaic aesthetic, Holland had a long tradition of topographical art, including such notable seventeenth-century painters as Adam Frans van der Meulen and Valentijn Klotz. Some critics were scornful of the topographically accurate, dismissing it as 'map-work'. In a lecture presented as Professor of Painting at the Royal Academy, Henry Fuseli contemptuously described them as 'the last branch of uninteresting subjects, that kind of landscape which is entirely concerned with the tame delineation of a given spot'. Topographically precise or otherwise, landscape had historically been consigned to the bottom of art's hierarchy. In the Renaissance, it was regarded as *parergon*, a mere accessory to the 'argument' of the painting. By and large, landscape views continued to be looked down upon; the 'mappy' pejorative persisting until the seventeenth century, when the consequences of the Grand Tour and the works of Claude Lorrain and Canaletto began to fundamentally change the reception of landscape art. The Grand Tour revitalised the cultural significance of the Classical World, inspiring generations of Northern European gentry to make the artistic pilgrimage south to experience at first hand the Renaissance and Antiquity, and aided by their art tutors, they drew, painted, and purchased architectural and landscape pictures.

An aspiring gentleman requiring an education in

the arts would study painting, drawing, sculpture and architecture, which he would draw, often with the aid of optical devices (as would artists). Trained in the art of technical drawing, their visual accounts of antiquity were more accurate than ones from the past. In Nicola de Martoni's *Pilgrimage Book*, a manuscript from 1395, the Parthenon's pillars were miscounted. More diligently, in 1674 Jacques Carrey ascended to the heights of the pediments in a hoist so that he could make precise drawings of the sculptures – drawings which contemporary archaeologists still use as a record. As was the practice, Carrey was the official artist in the retinue of a public figure, in this instance, the Marquis de Nointel, French ambassador to the Ottoman court. Two centuries later, the photographer Francis Bedford was commissioned by Queen Victoria to accompany the future King Edward VII on an archaeological survey of the Middle East.

Long had it been the custom for an artist to accompany an expedition, but with the Enlightenment, and the emerging Natural Scientists, there was an emphasis on exactitude and the empirically sound, and it was not unnatural for the scientist to also be the artist; the divisive dichotomy had yet to take hold. In each of the disciplines that developed, there emerged polymaths noted for their scientific and artistic achievements; figures such as the Victorian astronomer and mathematician Sir John Herschel, who was instrumental in the invention of photography and a respected *camera lucida* artist. Botany provided a perfect example of art and science working hand in glove, botanical illustration being a quintessential form of scientific recording. Many botanists were *de facto* technical draughtsmen, for example Joseph Banks, who accompanied Captain James Cook on his voyages to Brazil, Tahiti, and Australia in 1768–1771.

Draughtspersons would be a more technically accurate term; botany was a rare field in which women could play a significant role, although the patriarchy restricted many to merely initialling their work. The Swiss entomologist, Maria Sibylla Merian, painted botanical studies in Suriname on the cusp of the eighteenth century. Madeleine Basseporte was appointed the official painter of the King's gardens in Paris in 1741 and in 1759, Kew Gardens was founded by Princess Augusta, the mother of King George III, where Margaret Meen was one of the botanical garden's first artists and a mentor to other female illustrators. A botanist, Anna Atkins learned photography directly from the inventors William Henry Fox Talbot and Sir John Herschel. Employing the cyanotype process, Atkins made photograms of seaweed. These camera-less photographs, formed by laying a specimen on photosensitive paper, produced precisely delineated white outlines of the seaweed on the cyanotype's blue background. In October 1843 she self-published *Photographs of British Algae: Cyanotype Impressions*, the first book illustrated with photographic images.

Following in Atkins's footsteps, and the Victorian craze for ferns, Cecilia Glaisher made photograms of them, which were published as a portfolio in 1855.

Atkins's and Glaisher's quasi-scientific photograms paved the way in botanical photography, culminating in the plant studies of Karl Blossfeldt. Blossfeldt was a sculptor and art teacher who took photographs of plants as references for his students. Using a macro (magnifying) lens, he photographed botanical specimens in the most straightforward manner possible, emulating the example of the seventeenth- and eighteenth-century herbariums. This stark realism attracted the attention of the European avant-garde, and in 1926 his photographs were exhibited alongside African sculptures. Blossfeldt's aim was to depict the structure of the plants. Published in 1928, *Art Forms in Nature* established a matter-of-fact aesthetic that was to prove seminal in the revitalisation of 'record picture' or so-called 'objective' photography by art photographers in the second half of the twentieth century. There is, for example, a direct relationship between Blossfeldt's photographs of plant specimens and Bernd and Hilla Becher's photographs of blast furnaces.

A technical medium created as an art, photography evolved in synergy with science in the early nineteenth century. Empiricism found expression in realism. 'Painting is a science, and should be pursued as an enquiry into the laws of nature', declared John Constable, 'Why then may not landscape painting be considered as a branch of natural philosophy, of which pictures are but the experiments?' His predilection for rainbows aside, Constable's meteorological research, his sky studies, or 'skying' as he called it, attain a purity of depiction not found in his 'exhibition' paintings. As landscape painting became increasingly preoccupied with the specifics of time and place, the sky played a prominent role is establishing the season and atmosphere. The influential French *plein air* painter Pierre-Henri de Valenciennes counseled that the painting should begin with the sky and finish with 'les devants'. In his *Three Essays: on Picturesque Beauty, on Picturesque Travel, and on Sketching Landscapes* (1794), William Gilpin described the approach of maritime painter Willem van de Velde the Younger: 'Not many years ago, an old Thames-waterman was alive, who remembered him well; and had often carried him out in his boat, both up and down the river, to study the appearances of the sky . . . Mr. Vanderveldt took with him large sheets of blue paper, which he would mark all over with black and white . . . These expeditions Vanderveldt called . . . going skoying.'

In 1668, the polymath Robert Hooke presented a *camera obscura* to the Royal Society, recommending its use on expeditions to make accurate pictures. Topographical and architectural studies served explorers and the military equally well, the *camera obscura* accompanying the flagpole in the pursuit of colonial expansion. James Bruce used one on his search for the Nile in 1760. Of the nascent sciences, archaeology provided the perfect application for the *camera obscura*, as subsequently did photography; what could be more apt for a discipline focusing on traces and dwelling on hindsight? In 1819, the Irish archaeologist Edward Dodwell published the two volume *A Classical and Topographical Tour through Greece during the Years 1801, 1805, and 1806*. Dodwell was a Classicist and a product of the Enlightenment. He took with him a *camera obscura* and two lenses – one wide-angle, one long – and together with the Italian artist Simone Pomardi, they drew meticulous topographical views of archaeological sites, vistas and architectural details. Dodwell and Pomardi made numerous panoramas, for example from the church steeple in Corfu Town, or from the upper gallery of the Capuchin monastery in Athens. Their panoramas have the same formal qualities of early photographic panoramas: a foreground of splayed roofs giving way to a god's-eye view of civic cluster. The pen and ink panorama from the top of Mount Anchesmos is so monotone and intensely detailed, so replete with incidental and significant descriptions, that it feels almost as much like a map as a landscape. In an apposite history picture of his times, Dodwell made a drawing (finished in watercolour) of Elgin's men hoisting a metope down from the Parthenon, complete with the Reverend Hunt, Elgin's chaplain, busily supervising the plunder.

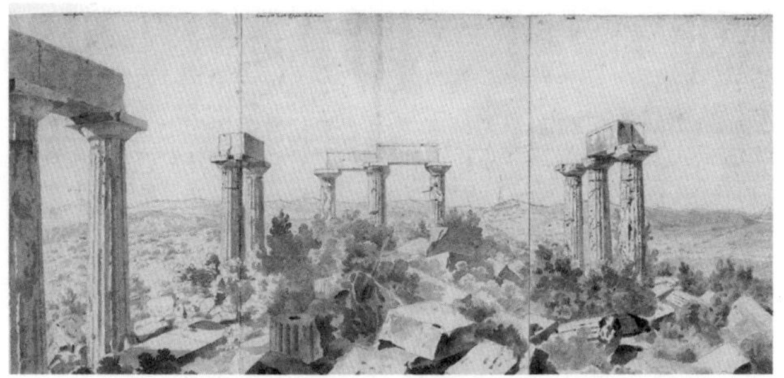

Edward Dodwell *Aegina, Aphaia Temple, Interior Looking West, at Mid-day*, 1805

Dodwell's and Pomardi's pictures are so scrupulously exact, archaeological researchers still use them to study the location and formation of ancient remains. Their mission was to produce 'Natural Science' records. In the marginalia, Dodwell would mark the compass bearings, place names (Slavic as well as ancient) and features, and a sign or the abbreviation 'Cam. o.' to indicate whether or not the preliminary drawing was made with a *camera obscura*, the hallmark of accuracy. He even indicated which lens was used, enabling the surveyor or cartographer to compensate for the optical effect of its focal length. Their pictures of derelict archaeological sites have an almost proto-photographic appearance. *Aegina, Aphaia Temple, Interior Looking West, at Mid-day* (September 23–26, 1805) is a sepia ink wash measuring 55 x 125 cm, drawn on a *camera obscura*, most likely by Pomardi. Isolated Doric columns stand silently as the harsh sun bleaches the stone carcass. 'No ruin in Greece is more rich in the picturesque,' wrote Dodwell, who spent three days camped there, to 'have sufficient leisure for the accurate delineation'.

Being of its time, Dodwell's realism was tainted by Romantic and Orientalist tendencies. For a variety of reasons, ranging from its lowly status to a belief that an unpopulated view held insufficient fascination, landscape art suffered from the curse of staffage. This absurd convention held that a landscape scene necessitated the inclusion of rural types, overdressed fops or lyre-playing fools; imposters who wrecked the paintings' pictorial integrity. These thespians clutter the foreground demanding attention, transforming a credible scene into a fiction. Staffage infantilises Sandby's topographical views and drains authenticity from Dodwell's records. The seated foreground figure in the headdress in Dodwell's *Panorama of Athens, from the Hill of the Nymphs, North of the Pnyx*, 1805 blots the view, enacting the artist's Orientalism. Devoid of staffage his pictures are revelatory; the others descend into costume dramas.

While some artists were inspired by the rationalist ideals of the Enlightenment, others found enchantment in the elegiac light of the Eternal City and the crepuscular paintings of Claude Lorrain. Although Claude's mythical settings have characteristics in common with the seventeenth-century *capricci* landscapes of artists such as Alessandro Salucci and Viviano

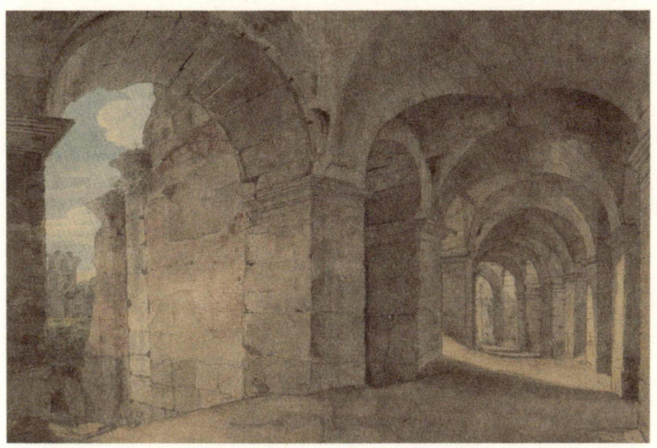

Francis Towne, *No. 21 Inside the Colosea,* 1780

Codazzi, the momentum was with empiricism. Canaletto's Venetian cityscapes were so precise, the Italian National Research Council is able to analyse them to determine the city's historic tide levels. When Francis Towne, a provincial English landscape painter, visited Rome, he saw in the remnants of a glorious ancient civilisation a warning from history, confirming his censorious view of the state of the British Establishment. Using a *camera obscura*, he made a series of architectural watercolours, depicting the Roman ruins factually for metaphorical effect. *No. 21 Inside the Colosea* (1780) features a vaulted gallery receding off to the right, an open view on the left exposing overgrown ruins under a wintry Mediterranean sky. An architecturally exact drawing of a series of arches supported by vast piers, the stone ceiling stretches away, curling overhead, enveloping the viewer, exactly as the image projected in the *camera obscura* would have filled the artist's field of vision. In Towne's watercolour, the sepia light and subdued shadows are as true-to-life as the millennia of wear on the masonry. Emphasising the fidelity of this artistic report, he records that the picture was made 'Decr 22nd.1780.. from 11 till 1 o'clock'.

Notating the date, time and conditions ('evening sun from the left Hand'), Towne often included the term 'taken on', which although in current usage infers use of a camera, back then had no such definitive interpretation; it demonstrates that artists were concerned to show that these pictures were verifiably 'taken from nature' on a specific day (and sometimes time of day) and not created back in the studio. Towne neither recorded nor acknowledged that he used a *camera obscura*, but a comparison of his compositions with how they would appear on the ground glass of a view camera (its technological descendant) reveals strikingly similar formal properties. My hypothesis was initially rejected by Richard Stephens, the author of the *catalogue raisonné* of Francis Towne, but to his credit, he re-examined his research and discovered a mahogany *camera obscura* itemised in Towne's probate. Prejudice about the *camera obscura* runs deep. Many artists were disinclined to reveal their use of such instruments whereas some archaeologists, architects and other artists working in more explicitly surveying mode, indicated their application of the *camera obscura.* The crude distinction made between art and applied art, supposedly separating genius from journeyman, deliberately takes no account of the nature of the commission, as this would unravel its fragile claim, and prejudges the picture, dismissing it on the basis of its diction. Placing due consideration on the employment of lens-based mechanisms helps puncture this hubris. The history of applied art awaits rehabilitation from the corridors of art's history.

Eventually, the artist's pencil in the *camera obscura* was replaced by the photochemical 'pencil of nature', in Fox Talbot's memorable phrase. 'The plates . . . are impressed by the agency of Light alone, without any aid whatever from the artist's pencil. They are the sun-pictures themselves.' or as Louis-Jacques-Mandé Daguerre put it when he announced his invention to the French Academy of Sciences on 7 January 1839: 'the spontaneous reproduction of natural images received in the *camera obscura*'. Here lies the genie in photography's camera; the ability to make an intensely detailed record instantaneously. But the speed and omnivorous nature of photography is also its undoing. The means to produce an image bristling with unforeseen detail is accompanied by a culture of haste and plenitude, the image receiving only glancing attention. It is said that Fox Talbot's friend and fellow inventor, Sir John Herschel, would have countered the claim that the photograph can yield an unimaginably intricate record, by asserting that in the time it would take to draw the same subject with a *camera lucida*, Herschel's instrument of choice, the artist would necessarily see the subject in all the detail that the photograph would subsequently reveal. Technology is a double-edged sword. Rare are the photographers who would spend three days with their subject in the way that Dodwell did, camped beside his ruined temple. Rarer still are those who study a photograph so scrupulously.

Photography straddled the ha-ha dividing fine art from applied art. Government, industry and the military were alert to its potential. Compared to technical draughtsmen, it was quicker, more accurate and cheaper, and surveyors could be trained to use it. Civil engineers appreciated that not only did 'record picture' photography provide the best possible means of documenting the progress of a project, enabling the engineer to 'superintend works they could only occasionally visit' but it also created pictures that reassured investors. Fox Talbot produced the first civil engineering photograph, *Nelson's Column under Construction, Trafalgar Square, London*, in 1843. Most of the early civil engineering photography focused on bridges; the first fifty years of photography coincided with the railway boom and its unprecedented volume of bridge construction. Daguerre photographed bridges over the Seine, Fox Talbot photographed Brunel's Hungerford Bridge, and J. C. Bourne and Roger Fenton photographed the construction of Kiev Suspension Bridge, whose engineer, Charles Blacker Vignoles, was also a founder of the Royal Photographic Society. In France, the *École des Ponts et Chaussées* commissioned Hippolyte-Auguste Collard to photograph bridge construction between 1857 and 1868 and in 1855, Édouard Baldus was commissioned by Baron Rothschild to photograph the Paris to Boulogne Railway. In 1851, in a domestic version of the Grand Tour *camera obscura* archaeological surveys, the *Mission Héliographique* commissioned five photographers to make photographic records of the country's architectural patrimony. In Britain, Philip Delamotte, Professor of Drawing at King's College, photographed the reconstruction of Crystal Palace in 1852, the earliest complete photographic documentation of a building under construction.

The needle-sharp definition of the daguerreotype made it ideally suited (its horizontal inversion aside) for topography and architecture. Carl Ferdinand Stelzner and his studio partner Hermann Biow photographed Hamburg in flames during the fire of 1842. The cadaverous shells of burnt-out buildings, protruding like broken teeth, are reminiscent of the pencil, ink and wash sketches of the destruction of besieged town of Grave by Valentijn Klotz in 1675. Each a form of record pictures, they share the same sober gloom of the awful 'that-has-been'. In North America, contemporaneous with the burgeoning market for lithographs of newly emerging cities, daguerreotypists such as Charles H. Fontayne and William Southgate Porter photographed panoramas of the expanding metropolises. In 1848, from the southern bank of the Ohio, they made an eight whole-plate daguerreotype of Cincinnati, the oldest extant comprehensive photograph of an American city. Imbued with the daguerreotype's amber and gold tones, the river burnished by the photograph's slow exposure, the sixth largest city in America stretches along a riverbank lined with steamboats and warehouses. Albert Sands Southworth and Josiah Johnson Hawes, as well as being Boston's high society portrait studio, photographed *McKay's Shipyard* (*c.*1855). Frozen within the metallic ice of the oval daguerreotype's silver-coated copper plate, its bronze tones and *repoussoir* reminiscent of Claude Lorrain, stacks of sawn timber are massed in the foreground, and behind them, a huge ramp ascends the scaffolding where the Leviathan of a hull takes shape.

An object of fascination and frustration, the daguerreotype was regarded as both a wonder and a means to an end. Depending on the angle of the viewer, the daguerreotype's image could appear as either a positive or a negative, and unless the camera were fitted with a mirror or prism, the picture would be laterally inverted. This inversion made it readily suitable for lithography, as the etching need also be laterally transposed. In the nineteenth century, catering to the burgeoning middle-class market, the onus was on reproduction and dissemination. Before the invention of the daguerreotype, this function was served by the plaster cast. The eighteenth-century archaeologist Johann Joachim Wincklemann was a great admirer of these casts, not least for their ideologically unblemished white, which emulated the Northern Europeans' Classical ideal, overlooking the inconvenient fact that many sculptures were originally brightly painted, and their blank stares from across the millennia would have faced us with implausibly coloured eyeballs. Anticipating subsequent, insane claims that the photographic image could surpass the sight of the original, Wincklemann's contemporary, the French sculptor Étienne Falconet, argued that the cast's plaster purity made it the aesthetic equal, or even superior, of the genuine article, and in 1836 the King of Saxony tried to swap an antique statue of a satyr from his Royal Collection for a complete set of plaster casts of the 'Elgin Marbles'.

Such was the symbiosis between early photography and archaeology, it has been dubbed 'archaeography'. When the physicist and politician François Arago made his speech announcing the invention of photography to the Chamber of Deputies in Paris in 1839, he foresaw its role: 'To copy the millions and millions of hieroglyphics [. . .], scores of years, and whole legions of painters would be required. One individual, with a Daguerreotype, would effect the labour in a very short space of time.' For all his enthusiasm, Arago, like many others then and now, saw photography, and specifically the daguerreotype, as a technology rather an art.

Countless daguerreotypes were lost or even thrown away, dismissed as studies for works of art. The career of Joseph-Philibert Girault de Prangey, an archaeologist and artist who made the study of Eastern and Western architecture his life's work, is a case in point.

Having originally trained as a landscape painter, Girault de Prangey had also studied lithography, an integral part of the process of adapting paintings and drawings into prints for publication. Although he submitted paintings to the Salon for exhibition, archaeology was his primary profession, and he applied his art to this cause. So detailed and architecturally precise are his drawings, it is hypothesised that he used either a *camera lucida* or *camera obscura*. In 1840 de Prangey learned how to use a daguerreotype and had a camera custom-made to fit plates measuring seven and a half by nine and a half inches, almost a quarter larger than the standard size then in circulation. He wanted to distinguish his daguerreotypes, which he intended for publication in scientific journals, from the smaller versions which would circulate in more general interest ones.

Over the next four years, de Prangey travelled through Italy, Greece, Turkey, Egypt, Syria, Palestine and Lebanon, taking thousands of daguerreotypes, returning to Paris in 1845. His plan was to publish one hundred prints in twenty instalments, but *Monuments arabes d'Egypte, de Syrie et d'Asie-Mineure* received scant support. Publication ceased after only six instalments; a mere 24 daguerreotypes were reproduced. Dejected, in a letter to Thomas Leverton Donaldson, secretary of the Royal Institute of British Architects, of which he was an honorary member, de Prangey penned photography's epitaph while still in its infancy: 'How heavy is the task I have undertaken, I understand it more every day. Our unfortunate orientalists find nothing, see nothing. For them, everything seems reduced to the experience of words, to pure philology'.

Girault de Prangey retired to Langres, where he had built an orientalist villa with a garden filled with exotic plants and birds. Isolated and increasingly estranged, he died on December 7, 1892. Passing through a succession of owners over the next thirty years, the villa and its grounds fell into ruin. In 1920, a distant relative, Charles de Simony bought the estate and discovered 'in a dark loft, a pile of rectangular boxes'. A daguerreotype is a magical object, its image a membrane within a polished surface, as elusive as a hologram. Like a dream that disappears on waking, a daguerreotype's reality lies sealed within; tilted one way, the steely depiction shows, tilted the other, the image's shadow-play surfaces. Unable to register the full spectrum between light and dark, overexposure leaves blue or purple in the skies and highlights, an effect at odds with its precisely delineated realism. Whether a consequence of heat and dust, damage in transit, or all those years in the attic, most of de Prangey's daguerreotypes are blemished. Spots and smears scar the pictures, the wizened surfaces sealing their hallucinatory appearance like the odour of ancient cellars.

Framed by the hills rising beyond it, *Monastery of Daphni, Attica*, (1842) shelters under a scoured magenta sky. Blotches of colour coat the highlights, altering its appearance to half photograph, half wax-rubbing. In the foreground, stones in the crumbled walls emerge from an undergrowth of scratches, like a partially visible face trapped underneath ice. So finely detailed does the daguerreotype record the masonry, it has the realism of a vivid recollection of the past. Its actuality conflates time; the eleventh century of the Byzantine monastery existing simultaneously with the nineteenth century of the wooden barn beside it; the viewer inhabiting the hour of that long ago day stilled within the picture.

Their spellbinding clarity is as lucid as a dream, the passage of time as distant and alive as a haunting memory. In a daguerreotype taken after his return to Langres, a low winter sun illuminates the Roman façade of *Porte Gallo-Romaine*. Under the branches of a stark tree, the street has sunk into brumal gloom; the copper rays lighting Caesar's arch offer no warmth. Dilapidated medieval houses flank the Gallo-Romano remains, their open shutters admitting the last of the afternoon sun. An elongated ladder leans against the façade, reaching as high as the top window of the adjacent house. Snaking along the bottom of the arch

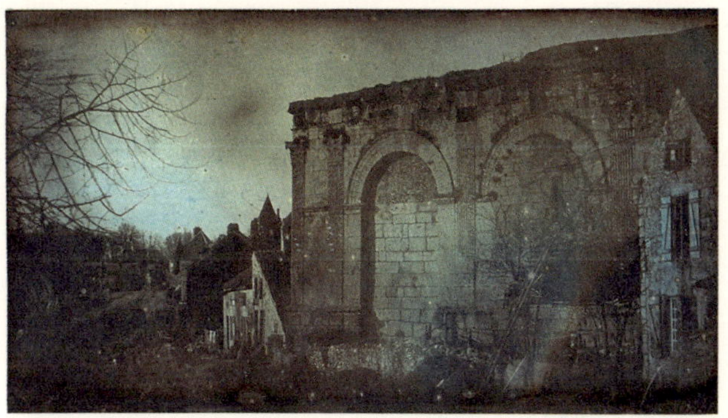

Girault de Prangey *Porte Gallo-Romaine, Langres, c.*1847

are the remains of a dry-stone wall, each rock eluci-
dated in the level light. On the far side, dwarfed by
the archaeological remains, is an oddly shaped house
with tall windows and a sign hanging over the doorway. Possibly an inn, there are several barrels outside,
and strung from its end wall, laundry on a clothesline.
Beyond, a cluster of buildings is already enveloped in
darkness, their chimneys and turrets silhouetted in the
daguerreotype's extra-terrestrial sky. A photograph
composed with the intimate observation of one who
knows the scene well, as de Prangey surely did, the
picture is imbued with an unconscious familiarity. A
conflicted individual, it is said that 'he would generally stroll along the circle, where his visits were unwel-
come; people dreaded his verbal attacks.' Whatever
truth, or exaggeration, informed this characterisation
by Charles de Simony, *Porte Gallo-Romaine* is a lonely
picture, a view of a settlement by someone estranged

from it. Such a sensitive presence behind the ground glass of the camera is rare, and his art, unrecognised in its day, is one of the great relics of the nineteenth century.

'Record picture' photography's recognition by the art world was an equally long road, stretches of which remain untravelled. The American Civil War photographer Timothy H. O'Sullivan is best known for his landscape photographs. From 1867 to 1874, the U.S. government's Geologic and Geographic Survey of the Fortieth Parallel covered a 100-mile-wide tract of land adjoining the transcontinental railroad from the eastern façade of Sierra Nevada to Cheyenne, Wyoming. Initially led by the geologist Clarence King, his team included topographers, natural scientists and magazine photographer Timothy H. O'Sullivan. Unlike archaeological photography, which looked back at traces of the past, these surveys' photography, along with that commissioned by the railroads, looked forward into the landscape. Beyond any scientific purpose, the commissioners' paramount motive was commerce; to facilitate investment in the American West.

By the time he joined King's survey, O'Sullivan was already a distinguished photographer. He had served his apprenticeship in the New York studio of Matthew Brady before working with Alexander Gardner on his *Photographic Sketch Book of the War* (1866). One of the most memorable Civil War photographs, O'Sullivan's *A Harvest of Death, Gettysburg, Pennsylvania, 1863,* was taken two days after the battle in which fifty-one thousand soldiers were killed. The day O'Sullivan arrived, the battlefield was still strewn with corpses. Composed with a shallow depth of focus to hold attention on the five dead soldiers in the foreground, the nearest one with arms outstretched and mouth agape, the photograph trails off in sepulchral definition, dozens more corpses prostrate on the ground, the living only vaguely present.

Cui-Ui Panunadu is the Paiute name for Pyramid Lake, situated some thirty miles north of Reno. It is famous for its tufa mounds, calcium carbonate deposits formed by an underground spring, one of which has a pyramidal appearance. O'Sullivan's *The Pyramid & Domes, Pyramid Lake, Nevada*, 1867, looks out over a tufa dome in the foreground to a diagonal line of them leading to the Pyramid in the near distance. In the light of a long exposure, the lake's surface is waxen, and tonally as pale as the *sfumato* mountains on the far horizon. The viscous lake and sepia sky create an unworldly setting, an eerie effect augmented by the tufa's bulbous shapes. In a reversal of the *chiaroscuro* tradition in Western landscape painting, the trio of dark rocks follows an oblique path across the luminous landscape but so detailed are his 12 x 10-inch negatives, ethereal sensibility is counterposed by the palpable texture of the tufa's coarse surface.

In the nineteenth century, when the technology was still rudimentary, it was accepted that photography's register was unable to record moving water or bright skies; these limitations were perceived as intrinsic to the new medium's astonishing realism. Only in hindsight do such aberrations detract from the depiction's credibility and cast the picture in a surreal light. Likewise, when colour photography became ubiquitous in the middle of the twentieth century, its palettes quickly assumed a natural presence, while in retrospect the artificiality of the hues is not only obvious but dates the photography to distinct eras.

When some of O'Sullivan's photographs were included in a show at the Museum of Modern Art in 1982, the influential art theorist Rosalind Krauss questioned their validity as art. Querying their *raison d'être*, she argued that only after they had been transformed into lithographs, and their imperfections corrected, would they be scientifically useful documents. This argument not only overlooks the ability of the natural scientists to contextualise the image (as they would any data under consideration) but fails to examine the photograph's minutiae. Comparing the photograph to its lithograph, she contends that they 'belong to two separate domains of culture, they assume different expectations in the user of the image . . . The lithograph belongs to the discourse of geology and, thus, of empirical science. In order for it to function within this discourse, the ordinary elements of topographical description had to be restored to the image produced by O'Sullivan.' Close examination of the photograph defeats this contention on visual grounds. O'Sullivan's large format photography allows the viewer to inspect the picture's details with a magnifying glass, its intricate description exceeding anything possible with a lithograph. That the vaguely defined water and sky lack coordinates is irrelevant.

Rosalind Krauss's argument is that this genre of survey photography is neither fish nor fowl; it fails as empirical science and not having been created as art, cannot subsequently be promoted to this arena. Her position frames the issue within the nineteenth-century context of 'exhibitionality' for the Salon or museum wall. Krauss draws a distinction between pictures explicitly composed as 'landscapes', consciously following the trajectory of the Western art historical tradition, and 'views . . . the term consistently used in the photographic journals, as it was overwhelmingly the appellation photographers gave to their entries in photographic salons in the 1860s'. View, contends Krauss, 'addresses a notion of authorship in which the natural phenomenon, the point of interest, rises up to confront the viewer, seemingly without the mediation of an individual recorder or artist, leaving "authorship" of the views to their publishers rather than to the operators (as they were called) who took the picture.'

While some of the geological features that O'Sullivan photographed were primarily of interest to the geologists, who often accompanied him as he worked, others featured the spectacular landscape

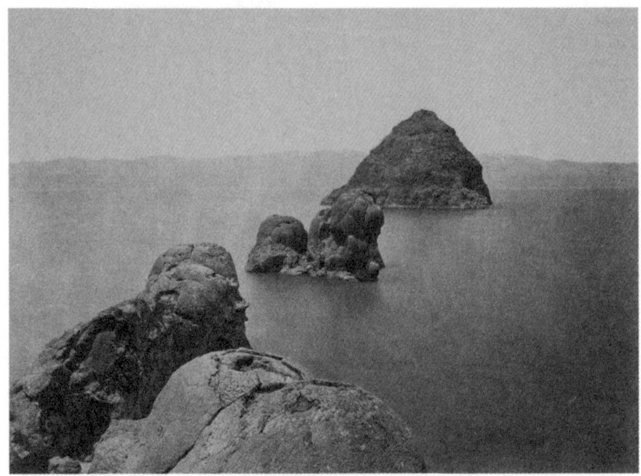

Timothy H. O'Sullivan, *The Pyramid & Domes,
Pyramid Lake, Nevada*, 1867

forms, as outlined by Krauss, for which Western survey photography was famous. A mile outside the town of Echo in northern Utah, a group of giant reddish-brown rocks are clustered on a steep slope. Remnants of erosion, they have the presence of the figures from Easter Island. O'Sullivan made a number of pictures of *Witches Rocks, Utah* (1869); close up as sculpturally solitary forms, and set back, as a mighty coven. In one, they lean back, imperiously, an effect he created by tilting the camera to one side. Whether his geologists approved of this artistic intervention remains a mystery, as does, rightfully, the mindset of the figure with his head under the camera's darkcloth, composing the picture on the privacy of the ground glass.

Prominent among these Western views were the photographs of Yosemite Valley by Carleton Watkins which were instrumental in Congress establishing the National Park System. Although Watkins is known for his pictures of sublime peaks and waterfalls, early in his career he photographed a mine; these 'record picture' photographs were later used as evidence in a court case. For much of his work, Watkins operated under the patronage of the Central Pacific Railroad baron Collis Huntington, and as in O'Sullivan's work along the 40th Parallel, the photography served the oligarch's interests. In 1875 Watkins went bankrupt and lost possession of his Yosemite negatives, from which a competitor made prints (a history unexamined by Krauss). His response was to rephotograph some of the same views, which he called 'Watkins's New Series'. He self-financed much of his work, living precariously, at one stage squatting a disused railway wagon. Watkins' life mirrored the boom and bust and scrabble for survival he witnessed in the West: the emergence of new towns and the devastation left by mining operations.

The stump of a large tree sits in the foreground overlooking *Cape Horn, Columbia River, Oregon* (1867), and beyond it, on the sloping ground, a tired wooden fence and shed lean towards the river below. Tall pines ring the hillside, perching on the crest of the rocks. The riverbank snakes away to a headland where a needle-shaped rock rises in harmony with the trees.

Watkins's photographs were hard won, and the best of them convey a sense of having struggled to reach his vantage point, and once there, as his body and mind settled, the composition created on the camera's glass rectangle presenting him with the picture's wisdom. In April 1906, by which time he was partially blind and almost destitute, a curator from Stanford University undertook to archive most of Watkins's collection from his San Francisco studio, but only days later the earthquake struck, and in its wake, the fire. A photograph shows Watkins being helped along a rubble-strewn street, smoke billowing behind him. Ten years later he died in Napa State Hospital for the Insane, and was buried in an unmarked grave.

Krauss's polemic suggests that these photographers were not artists because they did not follow the conventional artistic career path, and had no recognisable authorship or oeuvre. Numerous nineteenth-century photographers began their careers as draughtsmen and or painters; many others studied in the studios of established photographers. The issue of authorship is complicated. Photography rarely features the photographer's fingerprints, and the subject itself can be as much a part of the artistic signature as the composition itself. The photographer's style can be pronounced, implicit, or withheld, a form of style in itself. In 'record picture' photography, overt style is disingenuous, as it detracts from the sober clarity of the description. Nonetheless, often there are nuances which become apparent across a body of work when examined closely.

In her essay, Krauss cites the example of Auguste Salzmann 'whose career as a photographer began in 1853 and was over in less than a year . . . can we then imagine someone being an artist for just one year?' An archaeologist, Auguste Salzmann was also a painter who exhibited at the Paris Salon. The calotype photographs from his survey of Jerusalem were lauded in their day, and his panorama of the city received a gold medal in the *Exposition Universelle* of 1855. Continuing his archaeology, Salzmann photographed on Rhodes in the following decade, although these pictures receive significantly less attention. The Jerusalem calotypes are now in the collections of museums such as the Getty and the Metropolitan.

The calotype, or Talbotype, was invented by the eponymous photographer in 1841. Unlike his French rival's daguerreotype, which was a unique object, the calotype used paper coated with silver iodide to create a negative. Whereas the daguerreotype was known for its laser-like definition, the calotype was softer, and its tonal range more limited, yielding less distinct shadow details and textures. This aesthetic was regarded as more nuanced, more akin to a graphite drawing, than the steely-eyed daguerreotype. Grace of form trounced fact of outline. In the mid-nineteenth-century, lenses and chemistry were relatively crude; exposure times were long and depth of field short. In practice, this meant that foreground definition was commonly sacrificed for focus on the subject, which was often midway in the composition, an effect which gave the photograph a flatter appearance.

The purpose of Salzmann's Jerusalem survey was to photograph architectural subjects at the centre of a controversy. Three years previously, the archaeologist Félicien de Saulcy had returned from Jerusalem with drawings of remains that he claimed were from the era of David and Solomon. His critics disputed the accuracy of these drawings; Salzmann's photographs provided definitive evidence confirming de Saulcy's claim. 'Photographs are more than accounts,' declared Salzmann, 'they are facts endowed with a conclusive rigour (*une brutalité concluante*).' Quasi-forensic, their often blunt composition seemingly pre-empts Minimalism, a perception that has elevated their status. Minimalism and metaphor can walk the same path. *Antique Stairway Carved in Rock Leading to Ancient 'Porte du Fumier', 1854* is a vertical composition bifurcated by stone steps descending from bright ground level to penumbral depths. Positioned between rocks on either side, the camera peers in to take the closest look possible. On both sides, the foreground is left unfocused while the lens settles on the carved stairs. The contours of the top half, well-illuminated, are faithfully recorded in the calotype's embrace, while the lower ones only partially register; the edge of their treads are caught in the light, their risers subsumed by the print's dark tones. Early calotypes have an almost fumbling feel, their gauzy lines a ghostly presence. The faint aesthetic speaks in gentle but assured tones; understated, it invites the viewer into the silences.

The 'record pictures' aesthetic was given fresh impetus by the German *Neue Sachlichkeit* (New Objectivity) movement of the 1920s and the photography of Albert Renger-Patzsch, August Sander and Karl Blossfeldt's botanical forms. But it was the photography of industrial structures by Bernd and Hilla Becher that placed 'record pictures' centre stage. Bernd Becher was unimpressed by the photographic canon; he found more inspiration in an old gazette of local industry (the very photographs that Krauss dismissed). These journeymen remain largely unacknowledged; their pictures were commissioned as impersonal documents and viewed accordingly. Often anonymous and rarely found in the histories, these photographers are classified as employees rather than authors. Art history feasts on biography. The more fully-fleshed the narrative, the more the artist's oeuvre is enhanced, leaving the photographer in overalls to pass by unnoticed.

Bernd Becher's life encapsulates the trajectory of record pictures in a single generation. He was born in Siegerland, an area with a history of mining and steel production, and began by making technical drawings of industrial structures and landscapes, some of which he finished as watercolours, others as lithographs. By the early 1950s, many of the region's plants were no longer economically viable and were being demolished. In 1957, while he was busy drawing the Eisenhardter Tiefbau Mine, the bulldozers moved in, so he borrowed a 35mm camera and quickly took some reference photographs. Back in the studio, he reassembled the small prints into photo collages. Technically they would have benefitted from Girault de Prangey's expertise, and formally they were distorted with parallaxing problems, but Bernd Becher realised how much better photography would suit his purpose – a carbon copy of the way that art and industry switched from record picture drawing to photography in the mid nineteenth century.

One of Bernd Becher's fellow students at the *Kunstakademie Düsseldorf* was a classically trained photographer. Hilla Wobesser had been an apprentice in a large format photography studio and after enrolling at the *Kunstakademie* was given responsibility for setting up a darkroom. Hilla taught Bernd how to make technically and formally better photographs with a view camera, and together, they began photographing as a team. Their approach was a vindication of the fundamentals of photography. In the words of Hilla Becher, ' . . . the particular strength of photography lies in an absolutely realistic recording of the world. This sets it apart from all other image media; photography can do this better than anything else. And the more precisely it depicts objects the stronger its magical effect on the observer.' The Bechers understood that these industrial structures were essentially temporary, being built for a finite purpose, after which they would be dismantled. 'I became aware that these buildings were a kind of nomadic architecture which had a comparatively short life – maybe a hundred years, often less, then they disappear. It seemed important to keep them in some way and photography seemed the most appropriate way to do that.' Over the next forty years, working in Western Europe and the U.S.A., they photographed coal mines, steelworks, water towers, gas holders, lime kilns, grain silos, industrial façades, workers' houses and industrial landscapes. Painstakingly, they created a typology of industrial architecture, mostly from the twentieth century, some dating from the nineteenth century. It was a form of archaeological surveying, following in the tradition of the artists with their *camera obscuras* recording antiquities on the Grand Tour. 'If you visit a Gothic church, you have the possibility to go back to its time, to the culture which built it. Our photographs of industrial plants create the possibility of being in this industrial age.'

Their example had a major impact on the art and photography worlds, arenas which were historically separate but were beginning, somewhat warily, to intersect. As Peter Galassi, the curator of the Bechers' exhibition at New York's Museum of Modern Art in 2008 declared: '. . . in photography fact is the agent, not the enemy, of art.' At long last, the matter-of-fact property possible with photography was acclaimed for its aesthetic. The implications of this remain under-appreciated to this day, not just in photography but for the wider history of art too. Historically, photography has too often been critically praised primarily for its superficially formal properties, the elocution of the witness rather than the testimony. It is often conflated with 'easy listening', delighting in characteristics which simplify the composition into pleasurable contours. Photography is loquacious not lyrical. Accolades such as poetical or painterly are alien to photography's nature. Fundamentally, photography concerns content. Similarly, the topographical, archaeological and architectural paintings and drawings of the eighteenth and nineteenth century, derided as they were for being too 'mappy' or slighted as applied art, are belatedly being revaluated as art. The assumption that the merits of these prosaic works, however beautiful, rested solely on their usefulness and or charm as applied art, is (hopefully) on the wane.

Bernd and Hilla Becher were also instrumental not just in examining the language but the presentation of photography. They began with the conventional approach of showing individual prints in a line. 'There was a particular moment when we placed several cooling towers alongside each other, and something happened. Arranging them together in typological sets produced a kind of music. You only see the differences between the objects when they are close together . . . All the objects in one family resemble each other . . .

But they also have a special individuality [which] can only be shown if they are comparable.' So began what turned out to be their signature means of exhibiting their photography in grids of typological sets. Their inclusion in exhibitions of Minimalist and Conceptual Art introduced photography to contemporary art, a realm where it had previously been limited to a referent role and not a place for a picture in its own right.

In his role as professor at the *Kunstakademie Düsseldorf*, Bernd Becher was instrumental in the development of artists who became known as the 'Düsseldorf School'. Prominent alumni include Thomas Struth, Thomas Ruff, Candida Höfer, Andreas Gursky and Petra Wunderlich. Together, they formed a new group of art photographers who began making pictures based on the same aesthetic principles. Foremost among these early examples of photography recognisably inspired by the Bechers is the series of black and white street views by Thomas Struth. Quite large for its day but small by contemporary standards, '*Crosby Street, Soho, New York* 1978', is an 11.5 x 16-inch gelatin silver print. Looking north-east through the heart of SoHo's nineteenth-century architecture, the debris-strewn street, half cobblestones, half asphalt, glistens in the melting snow. A shiny limousine, at odds with its grimy surroundings, sits parked by a Stop sign. The city's daily roar has yet to awaken, but the calm clarity of this deserted scene breathes with the imprint of millions of voices and vehicles over the centuries.

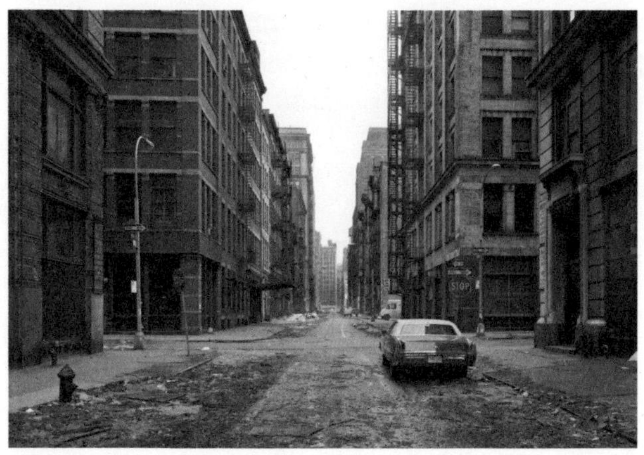

Thomas Struth, *Crosby Street, Soho, New York*, 1978

Taking a cue from the colour photography of William Eggleston and Stephen Shore, coupled with the resources available in Düsseldorf's photography infrastructure, the *Kunstakademie* students began making large colour prints. In 1981, Thomas Ruff made a series of blandly prosaic portraits of his classmates, which he initially printed and exhibited in a small format. Five years later, while working on an exhibition of these portraits in Villeurbanne, the gallery provided him with the necessary finance to enlarge them to whatever size he wanted. At first, he printed one a metre or so in size, but 'it just looked like a bigger version'. So he printed it again, this time over two metres high, and the results astounded him. Wittingly or otherwise, Thomas Ruff created something completely different. These huge portraits are astonishingly beautiful and defy easy categorisation. Passport photos with the presence of history paintings, they carry the weight of sculpture. Luminous, pale, inviting and off-putting, from a distance they look full of uncanny detail, up close they disappear into grain. This became a characteristic of the 'Düsseldorf School' colour photography in the 1990s; vast prints which could only been seen clearly from a distance, their definition breaking up on close inspection – a tantalising and frustrating experience. Inevitably, innovations in printing and digital photography overcame these limitations, from which new ones arose. They gave licence to Andreas Gursky's showmanship, his huge prints morphing into hubristic spectacles by the end of the decade.

The history of photography and the history of art might be woven together but the threads remain distinct. The 'record picture' photographs in Bernd Becher's gazette of local industry are a fading footnote. Every decade, countless archives of industrial 'record picture' photography are dumped; the financial cost of maintaining them deemed too high, their artistic and heritage value considered too low. Archives need to be conserved in their entirety, not only to preserve the internal logic behind their creation, but to sustain an original structure from which a myriad of interpretations can be drawn. When some of Timothy H. O'Sullivan's survey photographs were exhibited at MoMA, one of the objections was that withdrawing these examples from their original archive fragments the art. Singling out individual pictures is not the same as sawing panels from a Renaissance altarpiece, unless the photography was composed to be seen sequentially or simultaneously (as in a panorama). What should not be lost is the possibility of restoring all the components to its primordial structure, safeguarding its form and history. Dismantling an album involves physical destruction, unlike dispersing a folio, but both involve demolition. Meaning, on the other hand, is not singular.

As with any body of work – Edward Dodwell's drawings, Girault de Prangey's daguerreotypes or Carleton Watkin's landscapes – the artistic quality varies, and to only exhibit them in their entirety would do the artist and viewer a disservice. There is no more subjective term than artistic quality, and the weight of the curator's hand becomes more of an issue in the case of an industrial archive, which might contain thousands of photographs of varying standards. Long live the limitlessness of curators' perspectives. To chain the artistic license to the criteria that initiated the photography is dogmatic. The circumstances prevailing at the outset provide a socio-political context not a cognitive corridor for the viewer to follow. They are the 'once upon a time' at the beginning of a story, following a path witnessed according to each individual's autobiography.

Imperial Chemical Industries, or ICI as popularly known, was once the largest manufacturer in Britain, and some of the archives of its 'record picture' photography are now in the collection of Beamish Museum.

Without the funding to analyse and digitise this material, the archive is almost impenetrable. Largely dating from 1930–1960, most of the photographs only exist as negatives. This picture of a cooling tower under construction is one of the earliest in the collection. Its half-plate glass negative measures six and a half by four and three quarter inches, which I scanned to produce a 39-by-28-inch print, far beyond anything envisaged in its day. Hyperboloid cooling towers, as they are correctly called, are a feat of engineering; the ratio of shell diameter to wall thickness is proportionately less than that of an egg – only four and a half inches at its thinnest. Often regarded as emblems of industrial pollution, in reality they are heat exchangers, recycling water, and the emissions rising from them are vapour, not smoke. In 2020, I photographed some of these cooling towers with a similar camera to the one used a century previously, using colour film but following the same 'record picture' approach. The engineers who accompanied me around the power stations were initially bemused by the idea of an art photographer making pictures of these gigantic structures, but their doubts were allayed when they witnessed the respectfulness of the process. Some of them were apprentices at these power stations when they first came on stream; now they were overseeing their decommissioning.

In this print from the half-plate negative, the sheer scale of the structure is barely contained in the composition, the wooden scaffolding butting the top of

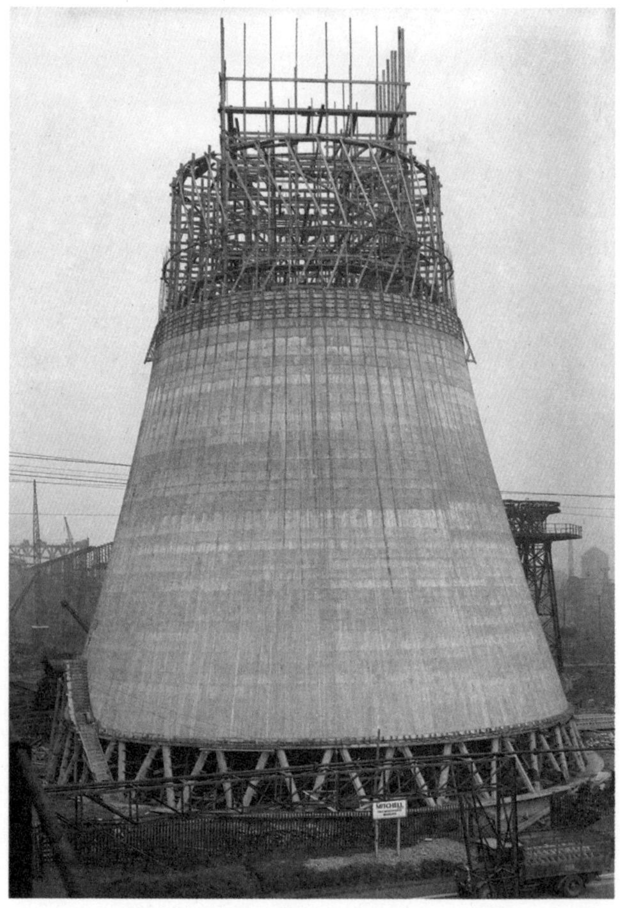

Photographer, site and date unknown

the frame and the circular base almost engulfing its width. A lorry loaded with sacks of aggregate waits in the foreground by some open gates in the steel security fencing. It bears the logo BDC and its number plate, VX 1141, is only just visible. Beside it is a sign reading Fred. Mitchell & Sons Ltd, Public Works Contractors, Manchester. A group of men in cloth caps stand inside the gate, possibly unloading the lorry. Propped up against the fence in front of them is a bicycle. The concrete base of the cooling tower containing a pond for the recycled water, forms a large ring from inside which the elaborate structure ascends. The tower's shell rests on a platform of ten-foot-high struts; when operational, air is drawn in through here to cool the vapour inside. On the left-hand side, a twenty-foot ramp, half staircase, half ladder, snakes against the shell's side, a two-man barrow resting halfway up. Behind that, half visible, is a steam-powered crane, its pulley wheel the height of a man, and beyond that a 100-foot-high wall of steel girders stretches back, past more cranes, towards a building in the background. The photograph's monotone emulsion makes it look like a dank day, and the men wear jackets and caps. Apart from some grass on the verge, there is no flora to indicate the season; it is a landscape of stone, steel and concrete. So faithfully photographed, the cooling tower's pale concrete is perfectly delineated, the graceful lines of its curvature elegant and sculptural. Two overhanging ladders are silhouetted at the top of the concrete shuttering, from which a maze of wooden scaffolding and steel reinforcement rods protrude.

Little would the men on the ground have known

that a century later, almost all these cooling towers will have been demolished. This is a photograph that looked into the archaeology of the future. A blight on the horizon that gradually became an industrial icon, the cooling tower looms up into the grey light like the last of the great whales. Conceived from engineering principles, the hyperboloid's shape is the pure expression of form flowing from function. This form of beauty is exact and uncontrived, as is the aesthetic of 'record pictures', photography at its most fundamental.

– The Family Silver –

One Christmas day, as the family slumped into their chairs after lunch, I unrolled a portable screen in front of the television, turned down the lights and set up a slide projector. As I fiddled with the focus, there was that familiar smell of burning dust on the projector's hot bulb and the smudge of bright colours on the screen sharpened, suddenly, into an astonishingly vivid photograph of our father sitting beside my sister in the long grass of a summer day in the early 1960s. My father had died many years ago and it was a shock to see him again, and to see him so young. The bemused atmosphere in the room turned into a stunned silence. My father is leaning towards my sister, and the brightness of her little white top alongside his pale yellow T-shirt, framed within the darker green of the grass and the deep gold of a cornfield behind them, give a *chiaroscuro* effect to the Kodachrome. The photograph's colours are rich and warm, and the focus is a little soft. My sister is putting something in her mouth and looks immersed in her little world. My father is facing the camera, looking towards my mother, presumably, who was taking the picture. The grass around them has been flattened and there is some paper beside my father, the remains of a picnic. He is squinting in the summer light and his mouth is drawn tight in concentration. His left hand is grasped around his shin to steady him as he sits upright. He was younger then than I am now, in his early forties, and his hair, combed back, is black and barely receding, unlike the grey and white comb-over we knew so well. I look at his left hand and his arm, and his watch, and remember what it was like to hold on to that arm, how I would turn his wrist to look at his watch. I stare at my father and like a crescendo of sound breaking the silence, in the glow of his picture a rush of my memories of him come flooding back; I remember his voice and the ticking of the grandfather clock as he sat in his armchair on a Saturday afternoon, the smell of his pipe tobacco, the way he crossed his right leg over his left knee, the heavy brogues he wore, the sound of him arriving at the front door. In the photograph, he is sitting a little awkwardly, looking slightly ill at ease, or so it seems to me, with what I know of him now. Sixty years have been and gone since that sunny afternoon and yet when I look at him in the picture, his presence is imprinted there so uncannily in the silver of the photograph, an impression as real as the flattened grass, it is almost as though it is not just the traces of the light that I am seeing, but an instant in their lives. In that stillness, I can imagine him breathing.

There is a blemish on the surface of the film which looks like a splat of muck, that appears in front of the picture plane, on the left side of my father's shirt. To notice it is to shift from the *madeleine* to the medium. Technically this is a colour positive; an old, archivally imperfect photograph, one of many hundreds of thousands, millions even, from an era a generation ago but now long gone. One example of a loose genre sold by the boxload on eBay and car boot sales. Prized mainly for their 'retro' qualities and supposed quirkiness, family slides are generally not taken seriously and are mostly treated as sentimental kitsch. This disregards their Proustian character and makes a fallacious distinction between an intellectual and an introspective engagement, as though the personal and political are separate poles. But family history and the human condition are bound up together, sealed in these tiny rectangles of celluloid slivers of actual instances in individuals' lives. The slides themselves have a protean identity, ranging from the sacred to the prosaic. These literally common-or-garden photographs are the fish paste of photography. Many second-hand photography dealers would sling them and sell the slide projectors. Physically, slides are an odd medium; two-inch square cardboard or plastic mounts containing a strip of film just under an inch by an inch and a half, which you need a light to see, by either holding them up to or against a lamp, or by projecting them onto a screen. Some of the rich vibrancy encapsulated in the film is lost in projection, although the great enlargement reveals details that would otherwise be hard to see.

Traditionally they would be printed as Cibachromes – glossy prints with high contrast, highly susceptible to fingerprints – but these reflected none of the lantern-like back-lit qualities of the slides themselves, and turn these amateur photographs into something rather slick, which is the opposite of what they are. Quite what they are is hard to pin down, hovering as they do between the realms of the tangible and the intangible, the celluloid and the projection, existing partly as record, apparition and memoir.

Photography arose from the art of recording an impression, be it tracing the image projected by a *camera obscura*, or capturing the light with photosensitive chemistry. The origins of portraiture, according to Pliny the Elder, began by projecting the shadow of someone's face and drawing its outline. In Corinth around 600 BCE, there was a potter called Butades, who made clay tiles. His daughter Kora was in love with a man who was about to embark on a journey. Wanting to make a likeness of him, she used a lamp to cast his shadow on the wall and traced it. Butades then placed a wet clay tile over her drawing and sculpted it into a relief, reputedly the first ever made. Kora's keepsake was preserved until Corinth was sacked, 750 years later. But the oldest portrait comes from prehistory. Pressed onto the limestone walls of a cave in western Spain, there are dozens of profiles of human hands from approximately 40,000 years ago, making them possibly the work of Neanderthals, and the earliest 'I was here' on earth. These handprints, made by blowing red pigment on their hands, (and mainly their left hands), reach across to us from the furthest edge of the ages, and yet they have the immediacy and presence of a child's handprint from kindergarten.

In photography, portraiture is a theatrical ritual, a dialogue, reflecting both the way the photographer was looking at the person, and the way the person was looking at the photographer. That direct thread is the spirit of the portrait. In the Scotswood Road area of Newcastle on Tyne, there was a photographer called Jimmy Forsyth. As well as documenting the neighbourhood before it was demolished to make way for highrise flats, he made portraits of the people there. They knew him and he knew them. One day in 1956, a little girl asked him to take her picture; she wanted it to give to her grandfather who was going blind. The sincerity in the portrait shines through. Her trust in Jimmy to make a faithful picture is evident, as is his trust in photography. There was an implicit understanding that the photograph was of her, not about her, and this is what he honoured in his approach. This simplicity, as naïve and sophisticated as the girl's request, is one reason why *Outside the Royal Oak, Scotswood Road, 1956*, has such presence. There is no poise, polish or hubris. She is able to be open to the camera without being subject to it.

The idea that a photograph can hold an image for someone who is losing their sight is more than a leap

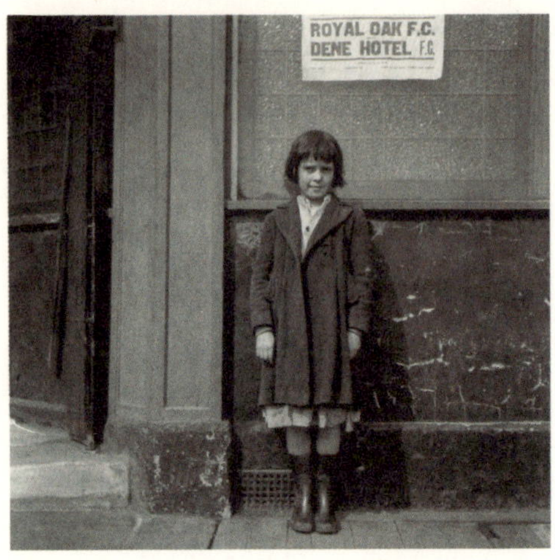

Jimmy Forsyth, *Outside the Royal Oak,*
Scotswood Road, 1956

of faith; it is a running jump over the fear of loss and forgetting. It is said that 'portraiture challenges the transiency or irrelevancy of human existence', a motive, maybe, for the handprints in the cave. But if portraiture rescues the individual from oblivion, does it depend on the identification or memory of the person being kept alive? What if their details disappear into the ether, leaving the portrait without a personal history? The finest body of painted portraiture from antiquity is largely anonymous. In the first three centuries CE in the Fayum region of Graeco-Roman Egypt, a culture arose where people would pose for their portrait to be painted on a wooden panel. These portraits were treated with great respect during the person's lifetime, and after their death, they would be placed on their mummified body. They are so eerily life-like, you could recognise the people in the street. Or rather, you could, if their pictures were treated as portraits rather than artefacts. These paintings are exhibited in museum vitrines not gallery walls; lacking famous names and conventional art historical provenance, they are regarded more historically than artistically. Similarly, Jimmy Forsyth's portraits are consigned to the local history department. The canon has a cold embrace; it does not accept people without an introduction.

Digital manipulation, retouching and darkroom arts aside, photography stakes its claim on the fact that what you see, really was there. As Roland Barthes defined it, photography's *noeme* is the *that-has-been*. This is the poignancy of looking back at an apparently factual image of the past suspended in an eternal present, a poignancy all the more onerous with portraiture, where the arrested past is the preserved optical presence of the person. Some portraits have more presence than others. Some impressions are fleeting, others more intimate – and some just want to be impressive, debasing portraiture into the service of publicity. The superficial depiction of status aside, what is possible or reasonable in a portrait? The etymology of portrait is the Latin *protraho*; meaning to draw out or bring forth, to discover, disclose or reveal. Here lies the dilemma and dynamic of the portrait; the nature of the photographer's desire to draw out the subject's character, and that person's response. It is a double act. Everyone wants to be understood, but no one wants to be explained.

The nineteenth-century French portrait photographer Nadar once said, 'The portrait I do best is of the person I know best.' Familiarity does not guarantee a good portrait, but it is a delusion to imagine that a photographer can make a genuinely revealing portrait of a complete stranger. The public face of celebrity portraits is just that. The private face in the family portrait is just the opposite. Whereas the famous adopt a well-worn pose, friends and family are more likely to actively participate in a more trusting, intimate manner. In many of the portraits in this book, people are actually leaning into the picture. From within the privacy of their family, they are exposing an aspect of their own sense of self that might otherwise be guarded. Only in the finest photographic portraiture are people able to be themselves. It is personal, for them and for us. Their look, their silent words, have the lightness of touch, and the weight, of a benevolent hand on the shoulder.

Launched in 1935, Kodachrome, the quintessential colour slide film, was initially produced for cinematography and home movies. In the US, the rise of Kodachrome rode along with the postwar consumer boom. Gleaming new cars, a kaleidoscope of new clothes, epic road trips to the National Parks, and the view from above the clouds, shone out from the living room projectors, bathing their screens in a Hollywood glow. The humbler British scenes, meanwhile, were projected in a paler palette of their own, more restrained than the vibrant American colours, more Surrey than Sunset Boulevard. There was no British equivalent of the American Dream; it would not fit comfortably with the socially conservative, fatalistic and self-deprecating society cautiously emerging from postwar austerity. While amateur American slides from this period exude confidence, British ones mutter reticence; the softly spoken tentativeness and hesitancy disclosing a glimpse of the privacy underneath.

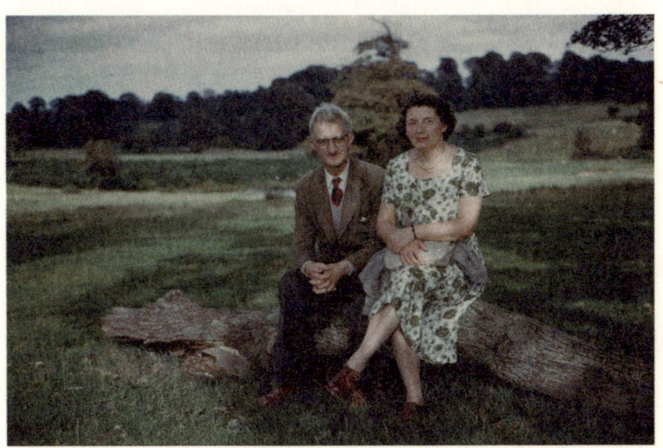

Photographer and date unknown

Family slides are often critically dismissed for presenting a misleadingly optimistic version of life, but families and photography are far more complicated than that. Forced smiles are patently forced. Photography is annoyingly and wonderfully awkward. It picks up on stuff rather than overlooking it. Photographs carry reams of small print. Its acute stare sees past the ostensible, bringing to light all those ambiguities that pretend to be private. From infancy onwards, we have stared at each other's faces, watched each other like hawks, forming our understanding of human nature. We are genetically engineered to notice. Photography magnifies this visual sense. It is like recording a conversation and then listening to it, hearing every pause and emphasis, every nuance, every hesitation, reading into the silences as much as the sounds. It is chillingly accurate, if unfair. Something slightly skewed, badly framed or clumsily caught, is there on the record. It might be what you said, but it is also how the photograph showed what you said, which is manifestly different. Photographs are messy; that is their eloquence. There is stuff in them which was not intended; the bits on the side of the picture – the hat and handbag left on the wall, believed to be outside the frame – the look on someone's face revealing more than the mask they thought they wore. In a photograph nothing goes unnoticed, especially personal photographs, which tap into the viewer's self-image and self-doubts. Instinctively, we are acutely sensitive to photographs of ourselves and our families. If to see is to look and recognise, what we bring to these pictures is far greater than any narrative could encompass, for we are bringing all our family stuff, all those yesterdays. All that is visible is but the tip of the iceberg; everything underneath comes to mind. This is why looking at family photographs is such a perceptive way of looking at photography.

It does no good to speculate how family slides ended up in second-hand shops and stalls, car boot sales, and, increasingly, on eBay. Some are carefully presented in indexed boxes, each slide's subject diligently captioned. Others remain in their film processors' plastic boxes, possibly with the year or event or place marked in felt tip on the lid. The vast majority are landscape views – parks and National Trust properties, beaches and other coastal scenes, castles, churches and quaint villages – places enjoyed on holidays. However well-composed and photographed, these views are largely generic and impersonal, but the portraits and more personal subjects are a private part of family history, and it is saddening to think of them orphaned and abandoned. For these are devotional pictures. They were photographed by the family for the family, often within the privacy of their homes and gardens, opening an intimacy to be honoured. Families would expose a roll or two of film a year. Each photograph would entail a certain ritual, technically and personally. There was no autofocus or autoexposure, and the photographer would have to use a light meter and grimace as he or she focused the camera. People had to wait and stand or sit still. It called for a concerted effort; the family pulled together for the portrait. For all the varying degrees of cooperation, bobbing on the deep waters of family dynamics, the single most important quality influencing these amateur family slides, the reason why their vision is so true to themselves, is their sincerity.

Whatever documentary value family slides might have, whatever record of a specific slice of British social history, they are primarily biographical. Their settings are as personal as the people in them; this is where they lived, and this is how it was for them. Whoever took a photograph of their roses without deadheading them admired them for how they were, some past their best but beautiful nonetheless. The picture of the Austin Cambridge was not an example of an era in post-war British motoring; it was their car, with their seats scuffed with their marks and memories. All those things which are now props in a retro-coloured costume drama were actually our things, as warm and familiar to us as our beds. The sight of them now is as loaded as an envelope with familiar handwriting, as full of presence as the creases on a cushion. Each is a biography written in the vernacular. From the fidelity of the badly framed to the awkwardness of exposed self-consciousness, they bear the evocative authenticity of oral history. What makes these photographs so compelling is their unassuming nature. They would never have imagined that people outside the family would be looking at them. To engage with these pictures

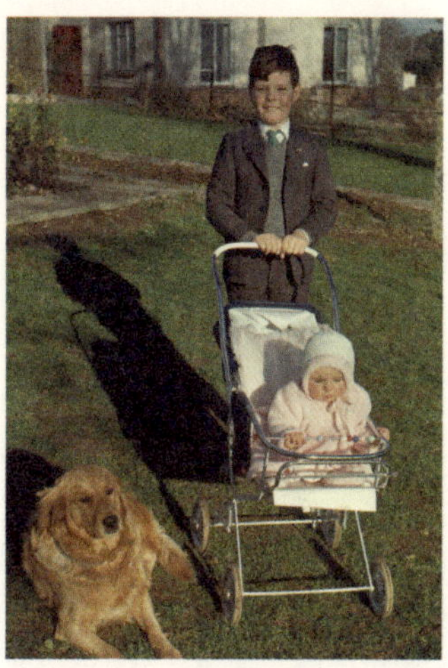

Photographer and date unknown

sensitively and introspectively is to enter into a bond with them; by admitting us into the past of these other families, they lead us back to ours.

These pictures are genuinely real and gently dreamlike. Part of this is due to their colours. These earlier slides had an inferior emulsion to the ones in the late seventies; their spectrum was smaller, making the colours warmer. Like the sound of leather heels on pavements, these are colours from another period. They are more naïve, more impressionable; they elicit a nostalgic response, they conjure a homesickness for the land of the past, and then they question it. The films' cruder emulsions were thicker, making the photographs appear flatter than the crisper, higher contrast ones that followed, giving them a warmth, a softness enhanced by the foibles of manual focus. They are both vivid and vague, part spectacle, part spectre, mirroring the fading of time and memory.

These are the shadows behind us, and they reappear and make eye contact. They face us from their homes and gardens, the kitchen door left open. The boy in his school uniform squinting in the late afternoon sunshine, his baby sister in her pram, the Golden Retriever outstretched on the lawn, their silhouettes on the grass, life's sundial lengthening behind them. This is the vanishing light of the golden hour of childhood, long gone but buried alive. That light's breath on the film's emulsion is inevitably melancholy, for every photograph is instantly a picture of the past, and far from capturing it, it is a look back at fate. That echo of a conversation held mid-air will always be behind thick glass; the photograph's scrupulously detailed depiction really is the roar which lies on the other side of silence. Those tiny traces of life unravel the sighs of our memories. Photography not only presents a picture of then and there forever, it does so without blinking.

– The Ship –

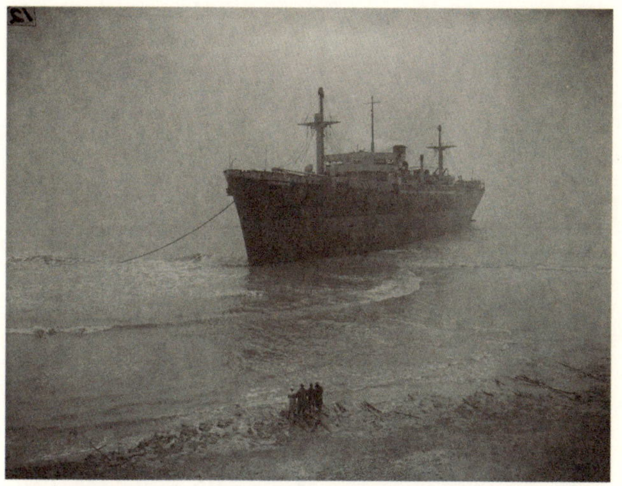

Photographer unknown, *The Kingsbridge*, 1955

The shallow waters of the Isle of Wight's south-western coast lie outside the busy sea-lanes of the English Channel. Dating from the Cretaceous age, the Wealden strata running along this shore is home to some of the richest deposits of dinosaur remains in Europe. In 2021, a new species, *Brighstoneus simmon-ondsi*, was discovered by a retired GP, who named it after a colleague and the bay, Brighstone, where it was found. Further along the coast, there are the three-toed footcasts of an Iguanodon. Formed 125 million years ago, when mud and sand filled the dinosaur's footprint, at low tide these two-feet square rocks emerge on the foreshore, seemingly heading away from the crumbling cliffs behind them, making their way back out to sea.

During the night of the 21 January 1955, a 7,150-ton freighter, the *Kingsbridge,* ran aground in Brighstone Bay. A tramp steamer, the *Kingsbridge* was sailing 'light' or unladen; even so, it took a week for her to be refloated and towed off to sea by several tugs. Ships lay up in these out of the way waters, either to bide their time, waiting to be loaded or, possibly, because of engine trouble. It is not known why the *Kingsbridge* ran into the rocky ledge at Brighstone; these waters can be unpredictable. Two days later, the Press Association sent a photographer to the picturesque scene. LONDON STEAMER ON THE ROCKS declares the headline on the little green caption pasted on the back of the four by five-inch contact print. Marked in blue felt-tip with the aid of a ruler, the outer edges of the photograph have been cropped, losing a bit of the sky and the shore but keeping four spectators in the picture. There is no credit for the photographer.

Being the size of the negative, the contact print has a latent quality, as though the intricate detail sub-sumed within it has yet to be realised. In this minia-ture version, the composition's arrangement is readily apparent, just as it would have been on the camera's ground glass. There are five elements: the shore, the spectators, the sea, the ship and the sky. Perfection is a term to be used warily in relation to photography because its nature is to reveal, and, if used sensitively, to honour, life's imperfections. This photograph's composition is so perfect, it feels as though everything fell into place. The shore and the ship and the sea are all on a slight diagonal, adding depth and scope to the picture. The ship is slightly off-centre, enhancing the naturalism of the scene, while the people are in the epicentre of the foreground, which graces the picture with an implicit composure. And even though the sea and the sky merge into a foggy horizon, it is level and true. This appears to be a photograph composed on a tripod with a spirit level and great care. It is unlikely that the photographer, whoever he or she was, ever saw a custom-printed enlargement of this photograph.

Printed to approximately four-by-three feet, expansive at last, the picture can breathe. Brighstone Bay is ringed by low cliffs, from which the photographer could look down on the scene below. Covering the sandy, muddy shore is a scattering of pebbles, giving way to flat clumps of rocks at the water's edge. Scores of thin black sticks or pipes, presumably jettisoned by the ship, litter the foreshore. Some are still floating in the sea; others lie washed up. The sea is so calm, the surf sweeps over the shallows in long undulations, some more ripples than waves, forming eddies around the rock on which the people are standing. Three men and a woman, the quartet stand shoulder to shoulder, looking towards the ship. Two of the men are in dark coats; one has his collar turned up. The woman is on the end, on the left, next to the largest man, who is wearing a mackintosh and a cap. She is dressed in a pale-coloured plastic raincoat with its hood down, and a white hat with a dark band. From the way they stand so closely together, they might be a family, or close friends. Equally, they might have been positioned like that by the photographer, to stage the picture in a reprise of a Caspar David Friedrich painting. Pictured here, they are *rückenfigurs*, 'figures from the back' in the terminology of German Romanticism, silently contemplating the scene, inviting the viewer to stand in their shoes.

The photographer's elevated position gives the picture an uncanny perspective, looking down on the people and up at the ship, in an angel's-eye view. The people appear to be less than a hundred feet away from the ship, an optical effect caused by a long lens, which for all the magnitude and space within the picture, makes it feel more immersive. So enormous is the ship, it creates a semi-circular wash as the surf breaks around its hull. Splayed over the shallows, this gentle wash adds to the picture's tranquillity, in harmony with the arrested motion of the waves, slouching against the far side of the bow. Dominating the picture, the immobile mass of the stranded freighter

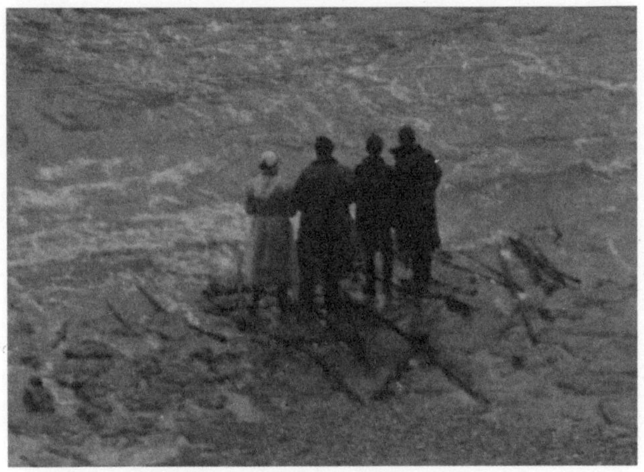

Detail, *The Kingsbridge*, 1955

fills the middle of the composition, its black hull rising above the shallow surf.

The ship's anchor chain is in sharp focus in the photograph, every single link clearly delineated. Even the numbers in the draught markings on the ship's bow, descending from twenty-eight to five, are legible. There was evidently a breeze that day, as the smoke or steam billowing out of the ship's funnel is blown seawards. Painted on it, only partially visible, is a huge letter K, along with two white stripes and a pale band, the insignia of 'Kingsport Shipping Company'. With its hull intact and funnel puffing away, the ship looks like the victim of a harmless accident rather than a wreck. There is not a soul on deck and a lifeboat hangs calmly in its davits. As such, it is more of a marvel than a tragedy; a sight to behold on a cold January day. Behind the ship, the pale sea recedes into nothingness, the horizon evaporating into the murky sky. It seems to be brighter in the middle, indicating a winter's noon time, and there are faint shadows trailing behind the spectators, which might be due to light bouncing off the water they face.

This is a picture whose time is set not by the hour but the decade. Created in those seconds on a January lunchtime, its here and now is absorbed by the weight of its dank history. As an emblem of post-war Britain, a rusty empire in decline contemplated by figures in macs and woollens, *The Ship* is a metaphor of damp hopes and faded dreams. The photograph's negative had deteriorated over time, staining its emulsion, superimposing little blotches across the sea and sky. This adds a layer of artifice to the image, record morphing into recollection, instilling in it an incontrovertible truth known only from dreams. I have lived with this picture as though it were an heirloom. They say that the *rückenfigur* is a lonely figure, lost within melancholy. But the *rückenfigur* never turns around; it is pure conjecture, each viewer's conjecture. I hesitate to write too much, for the saving grace of a picture is that it maintains its silence, and does not compromise the viewer's privacy. Like a dog that exchanges a knowing glance, there is an unspoken understanding. The figure in the mackintosh and cap is like my father, and this photograph personifies how I see him. He died over forty years ago and was almost forty when I was born; I was too young and unformed to have the conversations with him that I so wish I could have had. He spent two decades living in West Africa and India, in a society at odds with the emerging post-colonial world, and the life he found back in England in the sixties, even in the Conservative comfort of the Home Counties, had slipped out of register with his paradigm. All these years later, all too late, I understand that he was a *rückenfigur* too.

Sometimes I think I should keep this picture out of sight, even though it is my favourite photograph, but I find it comforting because it reminds me of him. There is great consolation in photography's sense of wonder and loss. Like the wave arcing across the middle of the shallows, wonder and loss is followed by wonder and loss, one slow wave after another. If you look very carefully, heading across the top of the sky from the left corner, there is a seagull with outstretched wings.

– Hoo Flats –

In the Ice Age, the Thames flowed across East Anglia and into the North Sea. Half a million years ago, as the glaciers advanced southwards, it was pushed downwards towards the Medway, sandwiching a wedge of land that still peters out into the estuary. This is the Hoo Peninsula. The road to its southern shore passes Hoo St Werburgh's parish church and runs beside some fields, skirting a marina and trailer park, before turning into a single-track lane that ends at a boatyard. From here a path, part of the Saxon Shore Way, leads eastwards, following the flood defence embankment as it winds towards Kingsnorth power station. Looking north from the path, there are arable fields, paddocks, and pylons. Climb up some steps onto the embankment, and stretching below is a bay with a salt marsh and mud flats. A jumble of houseboats in various states of renovation and disrepair occupies the western edge, separated from the rest of the bay by a creek. Reduced to a trickle at low tide, its streambed curls down the slopes of undulating mud before eventually flowing into the Medway. Here and there a yellow or orange buoy lies beached on the clay, a jolt of plastic colour in a landscape of browns and greens. It is largely a silent landscape, broken occasionally by the cries of the curlew, whose tracks pepper the ooze as they probe for worms.

The embankment meanders along the bay, its masonry overgrown and tumbling in places, eroded by high tides and fly tippers, whose refrigerators and kitchen cabinets are slowly subsumed by the mud and flora. Covered in saltmarsh-grass interwoven with saltwort, glasswort, sea purslane and sea lavender, the foreshore is pocked with little pools and fissures of water. Gradually the marsh gives way to the ooze, leaving isolated clumps marooned beside the saturated mud. At especially low tides, when the new or full moon rises closest to the Earth, the mud stretches almost to the horizon, exposing a netherworld riven with arteries of creeks criss-crossed by bird tracks. Looking seawards, in the middle distance is a small island with a circular fort, and beyond that, another small island fort. Almost out of sight, where the bay widens, there is the faint outline of a bridge over a distant salt marsh. Punctuating the view on the eastern flank is the monolith of Kingsnorth power station, the arm of its jetty protruding across the water. With the embankment of the flood barrier disconnecting the bay from its hinterland, the sweep of the bay is a zone of its own, made all the more mysterious by clusters of derelict boats bunched together at high water mark. Wooden craft from a century ago, they appear out of time with the concrete and steel of the power station, and the occasional clanging from the boatyard, and yet there is a harmony to the scene, its disparate elements coexisting within the ecosystem of the marsh and its mudflats. This is a landscape that revolves around the tides, regardless of the hour or the decade.

I found myself drawn to these rotting hulks with their elegiac beauty, but the sodden, slippery path to reach them has an equally treacherous antecedent in the history of the picturesque in art. Gnarly gates and tumbled-down cottages are a pastiche of art, numbing the eye and the mind, but the depiction of ruins need not necessarily be reduced to sentimental decoration. Photography is wonderfully disobliging, fastening on incidental details that a set designer would exclude, contradicting cosy historical re-enactment by including contemporary signs alongside older traces. Technical developments in lenses, film and printing have enhanced this forensic aspect of photography, particularly with large format view cameras, with their huge sheets of film and tea-cup-sized lenses. I revere photography's stubborn omniscience and its defiant rejection of the tendency to anticipate and summarise. 'Wait!' insists the camera, 'Let's really see what's there.' To photograph these hulks as diligently and faithfully as possible, to photograph the century's patina on them simultaneously with the uniqueness of that morning's tide – those blades of grass, that glutinous mud, the glistening seaweed – would be a vindication of photography itself; a picture of that here and now, forever.

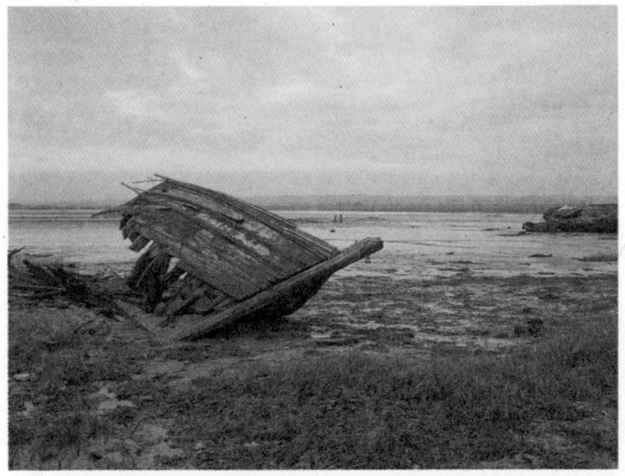

Michael Collins, *Hoo St Werburgh*, 2014

If the nature of a photograph is to ask an open-ended question, its onus is close reading the answer. Evidently, the boats had been dumped there because that stretch of the bay was away from any navigable lane, so they would not obstruct other passing vessels. Most of the boats, or what remained of them, were Thames sailing barges, used to carry clay for the brick and cement industries that ringed the Medway. Two centuries ago, Hoo St Werburgh's marina and trailer park were a brickworks (and the layout of the mobile homes follows exactly the delineation of the kilns and brickyards). The Medway's mud has a high silica and alumina content, and Hoo's is particularly rich. It was dug out of the bay by 'muddies', tough local labourers who worked in gangs. The barges would be run aground in the bay at falling tide, and a 'hermit', a strong, experienced muddie, would begin shovelling the clay into the bow of the barge, keeping the rudder free. As the tide ebbed, the rest of his gang would join in, filling the hold and then floating off on the rising tide. They wore long boots with a thick strip of leather to protect their calves on the slippery spades called 'fly tools'. Many of them lived in the nearby hamlets of Middle and Lower Stoke. They had their own pubs run by retired gangmasters.

Demand for the clay was driven by the expansion of Greater London, but by 1900 the number of barges had reached its peak, and the industry steadily declined until it died out in the early Sixties. In the hundred years of its existence, so much clay was dug out of Hoo Flats and its adjacent bay, Stoke Saltings, that vast swathes of riparian islands appeared to have been nibbled away. The introduction of mechanised diggers was the muddies' and the barges' death knell; these wooden craft were built to hold a hundred tons of the muddies' steadily shovelled clay but lacked the structural strength to cope with the machines' huge scoops. Now, the fleets of barges with brickyards stencilled on their red sails are extinct, their remains slowly sinking into the mud they were built to transport.

I would only photograph them in the winter months when the skies were overcast. In sunlight, the naked eye makes allowance for shadows, whereas the camera seizes upon them, casting them as *photographic noir*, emphasising the contrast, and overlaying the scene with melodrama. Overcast light provides a softer, cooler palette, with more naturalistic colours. After all, to take a careful look at the colour of a dye or paint, the most accurate method is to hold it in flat light rather than sunshine. I took my cue from eighteenth and nineteenth-century *plein air* painting: Constable's 'Natural Science', Turner's oil sketches, empirically observed sky studies, the Northern European realism of Nederlandish landscape painters. Artists who were out in the fields and forests, under the skies, faithfully painting what they saw. Photography's technical medium cast it as the Puritan in comparison to painting's Catholicism, but for a brief period, they flowered together as the Barbizon painters and photographers walked and worked together in the Forest of Fontainebleau. But this season was necessarily finite, for the *plein air* painters would witness the hues and shadows of nature change by the hour, while the photographers would be responding to the scene in minutes. In painting, colour became understood as light, and outline as mass, whereas photography delineated with light. As Stéphane Mallarmé described Impressionism's departure from the real, 'To paint, not the thing, but the effect it produces.'

On overcast December days, the bay is an elegy of brumal hues; pewter skies tinged with bronze and turquoise, blues and yellows, pinks and lilacs, the land a tapestry of earthy greens and browns. Drained of summer's vivid colours, the more nuanced tones breathe in the soft light. At low tide the mud flats lay fully exposed; the folds of the creeks, the tracks of the wildfowl, and the algae coating the sides of the hulks, all laid bare under the sober eye of the winter sky. Although elegant, the colours and clay form a melancholy scene. There is something unnerving and fatalistic about mudflats. For all the welter of unfiltered details trapped within the silver of the negative, and however matter of fact the composition, the photograph is never wholly impersonal. Subtly or otherwise, it is a reflection of the way the photographer engaged with the scene. This vista, however beautiful, is one of dank decay; this setting of moribund industry and decomposing artefacts, photographed in the months of shortest, lowest light, is composed with an element of winter in the soul.

Like seeks out like. Throughout the period in which I photographed on Hoo, in retrospect I realise I found the moribund scene resonant and consoling. Only in hindsight could I see the parallels between my life and work. Sometimes there can be an almost primal urge to take a particular picture, an urge best left unexamined; only later, when faced with the photograph, wondering why. To be too knowing about what the photograph will yield tames its feral nature, inoculating the uncanny, colouring in by numbers. For all the understanding that can be brought to the composition, it is only afterwards, when the open lens has asked its open questions and the plethora of light imprints have registered on the negative, that the full consequences of the exposure, along with the photographer's motivations, become evident. Hindsight is often conflated with clarity, but understanding is ever evolving, as are memories, reshaping over the years, shifting imperceptibly like the patterns of the estuarine mud. And expectations are life's obstacles and weather forecasts are often amiss. Sometimes I would arrive on Hoo to find that the cloud cover had burnt off or descended into drizzle. Sometimes I would arrive too late, and would find the rising tide welling up over the mud. Not every day would be grey, but those were the ones I wanted.

A photograph of a derelict hulk in a landscape will always be principally a picture of that hulk, however much attention is paid to its landscape setting, and the more I explored the landscape, the more of its mud on my boots, the more fascinating it seemed in its own right. Researching Hoo's clay mining history drew me to Stoke Saltings, the bay further along to the east which had been extensively dug out by the muddies. Stoke Saltings is a vast mosaic of a salt marsh perforated with clay diggings and a maze of paths snaking around higher ground. Kingsnorth power station and its jetties dominate one end, the Isle of Grain's power station and container port the other. A jerry-built marina of second-hand boats colonises the shore by the railway's level crossing, and avenues of power lines stretch across the adjacent fields, implausibly close to a microlight aerodrome. Although the periphery is ringed in all directions with modern industry – pylons, the Swale crossing bridge, fuel tanks, cranes and chimneys – the salt marsh commands the landscape; its banks, pools, gullies, and grasses giving way to the clay of Stoke Ooze, before finally disappearing into the Medway. Frustratingly, or appositely, there is no elevated vantage point from which to photograph this bay. It puts photography in its place. Hubristic terms such as shooting or capturing a picture expose the haughty superficiality that pervades photography's culture. It could not be more misguided; photography is a gentle art that is most sensitive when grounded in acceptance and humility. Much of Stoke Saltings is not traversable on foot, and lies beyond the reach of landscape photography, which only enhances my respect for the place.

By comparison, Hoo Flats is a smaller, more accessible bay. A few hundred yards east of the hulks, at the extremity of the salt marsh, is a heart-shaped promontory covered with sea wormwood that barely keeps its head above water at high tide. The land here is perilous; hidden beneath the silver-grey of the foliage's dense rug are scores of crevices and potholes. At its tip the salt marsh stands about six feet above the mud flats; its edges, carved by the tides, look like miniature cliffs. This provides the perfect vantage point and is just wide enough to fit the splayed feet of my tripod.

A large format view camera is a heavy object with a lens holder at the front, bellows in the middle, and an eight by ten-inch glass plate at the back, on which the image is projected through the lens. Its ancestor was the *camera obscura*, and it works along the same principles, with photosensitive film replacing the artist's sketch paper. The glass plate is smooth on the outside, etched with fine abrasion on the inside; this is the ground glass, on which the photograph is viewed and composed. In order to see the image clearly on the ground glass, the photographer's head is covered with a darkcloth. I had one custom made, five feet of fabric sewn into a tube and held around the ground glass's wooden frame with elastic. This eliminates all ambient light, leaving the image on the glass to appear in complete darkness – in a *camera obscura*, a darkened room. It allows me to stand back and view the entire image, or to lean forward with a magnifying glass, a 'lupe', to scrutinise the focus. Under the darkcloth, almost everything is reduced to the visual. Occasionally a breeze might blow the folds of cloth, or the odd sound – the cry of a bird, the bark of a dog – might pierce the silence. As the lens is moved in relation to the glass, so the image falls into focus, a kaleidoscopic blur suddenly taking on form and crystallising into a vividly clear image. Confusingly for a novice, this image appears upside down on the glass, but this is actually how sight registers on the back of our eyes;

our brain decodes it so that we see things the right way up. Given time to adjust, the image in the camera appears completely lifelike. For me, it is second nature.

Under the darkcloth, sight becomes heightened, and the vision on the ground glass utterly mesmeric. Everything is purely optical; nothing else exists. In the foreground, beyond the bladderwrack, the mud flats stretch out towards the horizon, the putty brown illuminated by thousands of rivulets reflecting the winter light, and the marbled sky crowns the watery landscape. Placing the lupe on the lower edge of the glass, I adjust the focus to the foreground. By gently moving the lupe along the glass, my eye floats over the saturated mud, wandering so closely around the clumps of bladderwrack, I can see its dark green tentacles glistening. I can almost smell them. I stop and finely adjust the focus, catching the glint of light on a wet rock. To stop my breath forming condensation on the glass, I breathe slowly, exhaling downwards through my mouth. This stills my mind and I slow down, stopping to look at a solitary rock as though I were down there standing beside it. Stray bits of flotsam stick up out of the mud – a piece of wood, a steel bolt – surrounded by trillions of tiny holes wormed into the clay by the polychaetes. There is a scattering of small stones, and on some of the larger ones, a thin coat of algae, a vivid green against the buff-coloured clay. As I move the lupe from puddle to puddle, I can hear the

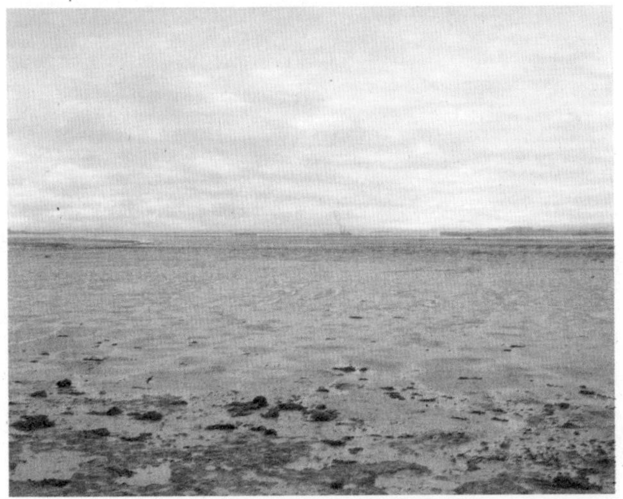

Michael Collins, *Hoo Flats*, 2016

sound of tricking water. Adjusting the focus further out over the mudflats, the pools of water multiply, the surface morphing from solid to liquid. This far out, the mudflats are almost indistinguishable from the muddy river, and the light bouncing off the water is the same colour as the sky. Much further out, a barge and a dredger are at anchor, awaiting the tide. Here the river widens, and sitting in the middle is Hoo Island with its little fort. Quarantined ships used to store their goods here. Now all it holds are a few steel lighters filled with concrete, protecting the seaward shore from erosion. To its east, close to Bishop Saltings, is Fort Darnet, and beyond that the pale span of the Swale bridge and the green smudge of the North Kent shoreline.

To compose the photograph, an extraneous frame is placed on the vista, eliminating everything except what is featured on the rectangle of the ground glass. That rectangle becomes its own entirety, its edges the borders to that world. However formally neat and pleasing, within that rectangle lurks anarchy, for what is envisaged as a still print is a photograph of a dynamic scene overflowing with details. That landscape is a world in flux whose elements – light, water, air, mud – are in perpetual motion, with such superabundance they surpass our visual acuity. So, the composition will always be compromised, and as such, composed with a human touch.

Unlike looking around through a lens, the image on the ground glass becomes a different manifestation of realism. The objects, the phenomena, are out there in the lens' field of view, but their appearance on the ground glass is at one remove, slightly abstracted by the way that what is visible is a projection of the scene on a translucent membrane, not the scene itself. This is accentuated by the manner in which the image on the ground glass is presented as a form of private spectacle within the darkcloth's theatre. Physically removed from the quotidian and framed in a rectangle, the image is beguiling. Observation and scrutiny give way to an almost trance-like wonder, the projection of the landscape morphing into metaphor, disassociated details triggering mnemonic trails. These are those rare occasions when the spell is so enveloping, the traffic in my brain dies down, bringing me to a pre-linguistic state where emotions remain unchristened. All those thoughts and feelings, all that heart, more than can ever be described or explained, are set free in photography's vow of silence.

When taking a picture with a view camera, a sheet of film is inserted into the back, just inside the ground glass. This means that unlike most cameras, you cannot look through the lens when you are exposing the film. Instead, the photographer stands by the side, cable release in hand, watching and waiting for the right moment. Waiting for some birds to fly past or waddle off, or for a passing yacht that would be blurred by the camera's slow exposure. Although nothing compares to looking at the ground glass under the darkcloth, waiting with the cable release is the most intense part of the process. Each exposure is very expensive, and these large sheets of film should be used sparingly. So, with my thumb on the button I would wait, watching out for wildfowl, keeping an eye on the breeze, listening to the trickling sound of the tide. Pressing the button would be a culmination of that day's hopes and efforts, of getting there to find the right light and sky, of hauling the heavy camera equipment over the spongey ground. But most of all it would feel like opening the lens to something idealistic and naïve. To a childlike hope and wonder, to trying to make something sincere and as such, beautiful. Distinct from my pictures of the hulks, these photographs are pointing forwards, out to the horizon over Hoo Flats. Although photography is innately retrospective – every exposure is instantly a record of the past – these particular landscapes have a Janusian quality, as they face ahead to open water, where the river meets the sky. I never tired of photographing Hoo Flats, and returned again and again, until eventually the vantage point crumbled into the bay.

– Blind Corners –

It was the label that caught my eye. They were on a stall along with hundreds of old photographs, postcards and cameras, and came in a shallow, grey cardboard box that was falling apart. Pasted on its lid, in faded black ink, the description read 'Negs: of Blind Corners'. Someone had underlined it in pencil. Inside, under a sheet of glassine paper, was a dozen six-and-a-half by eight-and-a-half-inch glass negatives. I took one out of the box and held it to the light, under the stall-holder's wary look. It showed an empty street scene. Without even needing to negotiate, I bought the box for a song. Back home, I inspected these 'full plate' negatives on a lightbox. Some had scratches or chips, others had strange blemishes. There were traces of captions in ruddy ink on the edge of the glass, mostly reduced to illegible blobs, only some dates remained; they were taken in the mid-1920s. Over the years, their emulsion had faded, leaving it increasingly thin at the edges, like dried-up puddles with dark mud in the middle, faint residue around the periphery. I tried scanning them, but they were so damaged, the results were tantalisingly disappointing.

Not having the skill to digitally restore the photographs, I placed the negatives in an archival box and consigned them to a work in progress shelf. Every now and again I would wonder about them; a long-unanswered letter awaiting a reply. Years later, I began working with an excellent digital retoucher who was intrigued by these mysterious negatives and asked me to send him high resolution scans. Two of the negatives would have required so many hours' work, they would be too costly to salvage, but the others were restored to the same – if not superior – exposures that emerged from the chemicals of the photographer's darkroom a century ago. As pristine as the day they first saw daylight, they look slightly unreal, like a great grandfather with ivory-white teeth.

The ten photographs were all classically composed, Claude Lorrain style, with an open foreground flanked by structures either side, although rather than arcadian silviculture and dilapidated Doric columns, there are tarred macadam streets bordered by stone walls, garden fences, shop fronts and trees. Each picture follows the same pattern; the photographer had placed his (almost certainly his) tripod in the middle of the road, looking straight ahead, the blind corners disappearing off to the sides, making the composition both formally pleasing and enigmatic. So, although each location is seemingly laid bare in the clear light, overarching the finely detailed quotidian scenes is the unseen. A vacant, unremarkable stretch of road fills the foreground, as clear as glass, while only the beginnings of the side

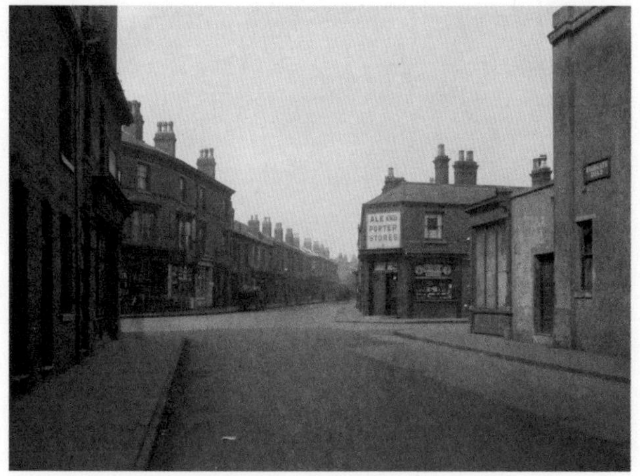

Photographer and site unknown, *c.*1924

roads are visible; where they lead to and what lurks beyond is withheld from view. Photographed in winter, the filigree of the trees' bare branches is minutely etched against the black and white film's featureless grey skies, a blank aspect common to all the pictures that gives them a slightly surreal tone. Some scenes are completely empty of people, others have the odd figure; a woman in a long coat with a thick collar and matching hat choosing vegetables outside the greengrocer's; a man in a trilby standing by a lamp post; a postman on a bicycle, picked out perfectly against the white wall behind him, who has stopped to look at the proceedings; the driver of a horse and cart, come to a stop, as has the man in the dark suit on the pavement beside them. The necessarily long exposure times of the large format photography has rendered anything or anyone that was moving slightly blurred, but still recognisable. Like a double exposure, a hazily defined horse and cart clops towards us, while on the pavement beside a post box, barely visible is a wraithlike woman, two black legs under a smudged black coat. The longer I look, the more an initial impression of an empty street fades.

They were evidently a set of photographs commissioned by a local authority's highways department to document a series of blind corners so the planners could see what road safety modifications were required. The roads' rounded corners, designed to accommodate the wide turning arc and slow speed of a horse and cart, were now motor car accidents waiting to happen. Classified as 'record pictures', this genre of photography is characterised by its matter-of-fact aesthetic; a seemingly naturalistic depiction free from contorted perspectives, stylistic excesses, or blunt polemic, meaning that any metaphorical effects are drawn from the photograph rather than being imposed within it. Of course, the dichotomy between natural and contrived is false; nothing is natural, we each hallucinate reality and everything has its own style. That the good burghers with their Ministry of Transport manuals commissioned and inspected these photographs with such a specific agenda does not dictate their 'ultimate meaning', as Roland Barthes argued in *The Death of the Author*. The record pictures' apparently deadpan verisimilitude resists the confines of a set interpretation.

Free from inflection, the aesthetic offers each viewer a *tabula rasa*. Context can insist meaning, but that is only one voice; these newly digitised photographs, available in various forms and sizes unimaginable in their day, are not bound by their original imprimatur. This is not to deny or disguise the photography's foundational function, but it is only one consideration among many, and not necessarily the most fertile.

Zooming further and further into the digitised photographs, it's possible to read several street signs and in one, mounted on an old lamp post, a signpost pointing to Great Barr and, in the opposite direction, Birmingham. There are two pairs of photographs, each taken from adjacent streets. In one, at a crossroads, which appears to be in the heart of the village, there is an off-licence. Ale and Porter Stores is right on the corner, its boldly painted façade facing the convergence of the roads. It has a window displaying all kinds of bottles, as well as signs for Ansell's Bitter Beer and Gilbey's Invalid Port, a brand that was advertised, and even prescribed, as a tonic. Its doors have the same kind of acid-etched decorative windows you'd find in a pub, and the right hand one is ajar. Opposite the off-licence is the grocer's with the lady rummaging through the vegetables. Strung above her is a row of rabbits. Enlarged even further, only her shoes remain distinct – so blurred is the figure, there might even be two of them – and over her shoulder is the diaphanous trail of what must have been another person's presence, who on closer examination, turns out to have been standing in front of her. The solid details of the tobacconist's next door and the ornate brickwork of the shop in the foreground coexist with these spectral vestiges, ghosts of time past inhabiting these pictures' history.

Photography is all about spectral vestiges and blind corners. Called the optical unconscious, this is a poly-semically nebulous term. Coined by Walter Benjamin in his 1931 essay 'A Short History of Photography', initially his perspective focused on the philosophical implications of being able to see phenomena previously invisible without the technology of slow motion or enlargement – the bodies in motion studies by Edweard Muybridge or Karl Blossfeldt's hugely magnified photographs of botanical specimens. 'It is through photography that we first discover the existence of this optical unconscious, just as we discover the instinctual unconscious through psychoanalysis.' Five years later, in his second version of 'The Work of Art in the Age of its Technological Reproducibility', Benjamin extended the concept of the optical unconscious to embrace photography's impact on the unconscious: 'The ancient truth expressed by Heraclitus, that those who are awake have a world in common while each sleeper has a world of his own, has been invalidated by film – and less by depicting the dream world itself than by creating figures of collective dreams, such as the globe-encircling Mickey Mouse.'

Benjamin drew on the concept of the latent image from Sigmund Freud's *The Interpretation of Dreams*, although his focus was on capitalism's 'dream-world'. Freud often employed photography as an analogy, comparing an unrecalled early childhood memory to a photograph's unprinted negative. But with photography it works the other way round; the mnemonic portals uncovered within the picture's realism lead back to the mists of the individual's past. However, it is Freud's concept of the uncanny, when something familiar or ordinary provokes a feeling of unease, that touches on the subliminal aspect of these banal photographs of blind corners. Photography's realism is so instinctively credible, its fingerprint-level forensics have all the believability of a dream. We fashion its facts into our narratives. Because there is nothing synthetic in a record picture's realism, it can tap into a sense of the 'secretly familiar', that disquieting astonishment that Freud believed was triggered by repressed memories, taboos and such like. This feeling of recognition need not necessarily be traumatic; the viewer's immersion in the quotidian realism of the blind corners might morph into less troubled memories of pavements and paths from the past, circumstances recalled from long ago or imagined from family lore, glimpses from the unconscious floating up to the surface.

I have little motivation to identify the precise location of these blind corners, or to compare them to their contemporary conditions, because the past is another village long since lost to colonisation by cars and consumerism and my interest is in the petrified history contained within them. A lamp post sits at the junction of Wheelwright Road and Huntun Hill, the sharp shape of its glass lamp picked out in the faintly raking winter light. Surmounted by an ornate cupola with vents, it was originally gas-lit but might have been converted to electricity. Although taken in the mid-1920s, the scene in the photograph encompasses several decades and eras, from gas to electricity and beyond. Propped up against the street sign for Huntun Hill, mounted on a board, is an advertisement for a local event. The fourth annual demonstration is due to be held at the church house on 24 March 24, but quite what this demonstration will be is indecipher-able. Despite its setting, it seems to be secular rather than religious.

Not a soul stirs. The crossroad is bordered by a series of high masonry walls, some topped with hedges, asserting the privacy of the large houses with their gardens. The photograph looks as though it was taken in the morning just as the mist was burning off. In the distance, as Wheelwright Road curves out of sight, the houses become hazy. There are cobblestones on the left-hand edge of Wheelwright Road, and an item of litter (old newspaper?), and in the middle, some flattened horse dung. Attached to the base of the lamp post is a wire bin containing scrunched-up balls of paper. Picked out by the low sun, the metal lamp post

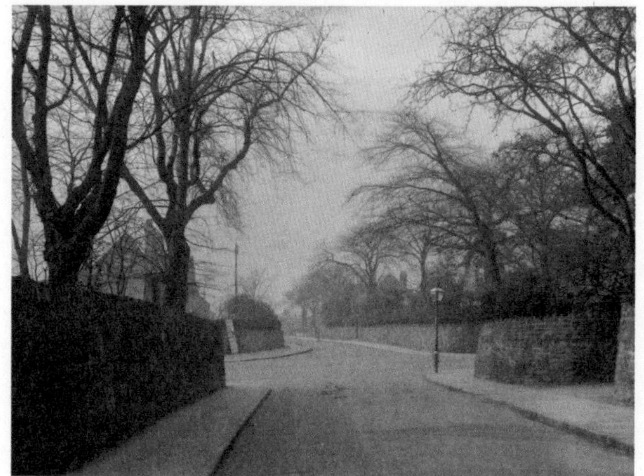

Photographer and site unknown, *c.*1924

stands out in profile against the smooth stone walls and unmarked surface of the road, a counterpoint to the graceful timelessness of the scene. Peace prevails. In an upstairs window of a grand Victorian house the curtains are half drawn. Soft shadows from the walls and trees sweep across the picture from the left, their diaphanous forms shading the foreground, as the rubblestone walls on the right-hand side glow in the wispy sunlight.

The composition's form – a road bifurcated by truncated arms either side – establishes a template that runs through this series of blind corner photographs, an underlying rhythm conjoined with its multiple variations of the built environment. Testament to these photographs' *raison d'être*, the compositions hang on this framework, illustrating a satisfying sense of pragmatism. Photography is the most garrulous medium – the film's emulsion (or digital sensor) is a magnet for absolutely all and sundry – and form is the melody that enfolds this seething content. Form is both a superficial view and a fundamental one; it's a picture's geological structure and its most overt feature. Too ostentatious, it muffles the content; too vague, and the picture collapses under its own weight. Form is the armchair that seduces the viewer to sit back and look. Detail is what makes the viewer lean forward.

Wheelwright's thick stone walls and wide roads lie heavily on the bottom third of the composition, anchoring the scene as the trees stretch upwards, holding them firmly in their place as their trunks and boughs and branches well up from the gardens, filling the space and sky with their tendrils. On the right-hand side, lit in the soft light in a subtle array of greys, the trees lean towards the road, almost arching, sculptural and muscular, and even the tiniest twigs at the end of the thinnest branches are recorded with the precision of a Renaissance silverpoint. The ones in the foreground have a tactile presence – reach out and you can feel the coarse skin of their bark on the palm of your hand – along with the odour of the damp earth and its evergreen hedge. Further back, in the epicentre of the composition, the exquisite finery of the branches curls and weaves, fading from view at the bend of the road.

On the left-hand side, slightly *contre-jour*, the trees are dark against the sky. Cold, stark, ominous shapes with sawn boughs and dead branches, their presence feels more immediate; they have a breath rather than a scent. These trees creak and groan. The stone wall is in shadow. It's cold on this side; there's no warmth. On the corner, where the wall ends, there's the back of another sign, a noticeboard mounted on stakes. The house visible behind it is plainer than the one facing it from across the road. It is a picture of two halves divided by the light; the side in the light is comforting while the other is faintly disturbing. One side sighs, the other mutters.

And yet, overall, the form has such harmony and is undeniably graceful. The warmth of the soft light, the smooth curves of the stone walls, the comfort of worn paving stones, the sanctuary of the houses with their gables, the natural beauty of the trees' latticework, the serenity of the empty streets: an image extolling the virtues and reassurance of suburban England. But contrasting with such a halcyon ideal, the junction of Wheelwright Road and Hunton Hill was regarded as hazardous; this picture depicts danger. There must have been accidents – possibly fatal – for this blind corner to be brought to the committee's attention. The silence of those smooth roads might have been pierced by screams and soaked in blood. Or possibly the screech of brakes accompanied by coarse oaths. Less dramatically but equally deathly, even the most banal association can resonate with an individual's psyche. The original title of Freud's essay 'The Uncanny' was the corresponding German term '*das Unheimlich*', a noun which is also the antonym of homely. Leaning forward into the picture, standing in the middle of Wheelwright Road in that patch of sunshine, a dreadful sense of familiarity sinks in. An exclusion zone of implacable stone walls and private driveways, with blind corners on both sides, suspended in silence.

Nothing is moving in Wheelwright Road. Time's second hand has been stopped. Historically, in *plein air* paintings and drawings, artists would depict the shadows, partly in the name of realism, to illustrate the hour of the day and metaphorically to signify the passage of time. The snap of the shutter in photography makes this its death mask. Photography is inherently melancholic because of our innate sense that what we can see in the instant of the exposure has inexorably passed away. Its magical promise to behold that moment in time comes at great cost, as does any deal with the gods. Photography's realism is tinged with fatalism. The timeless beauty of Wheelwright Road has a terminal disease. A century on, all those elegant elm trees would have died, poisoned by a fungus that arrived here that same decade. Nothing would remain of their sylvan canopy; the stone walls would dominate today's vista.

Photography is known as the art of fixing a shadow, but nothing is fixed, not least meaning. It's wishful to look to photography for certainty, because the light in its exposure is an explosion of consciousness, rambling off script, garrulous and unfiltered, leaving a swathe of complexities and contradictions in its wake. Photography is the medium of dialectics. Everyone sees something slightly (or significantly) different in the picture, from the diverse members of the highways planning committee onwards. (And did anyone ever ask the journeyman photographer?) Rather than clarifying, it complicates. Photography is a long-winded answer unrestrained by the question.

Photography is by nature a literal art, indexical to a fault. It is an instantaneous stream of consciousness. Submerged within its traces are more traces. But these traces are not clues; there is no conclusive narrative. Photography doesn't require imagination; memory is its oxygen. The bitter irony is that photography, an art form that has been pimped to death, is actually the medium of introspection. Photography is not *this* here and now, it's *that* here and now; a past at one remove that never goes away, an atemporal vantage point of a moment in time. Hindsight polishes retrospect's lens. The longer the interval between then and now, the more the depths emerge in the picture. Warning: blind corners.

NOTES

Personal Picture Show

p. 42 *they'd go there by the dozens*: Julia Scully, *Disfarmer: The Heber Springs Portraits, 1939–1946: From the Collections of Peter Miller and Julia Scully* (Danbury: Addison House, 1976), pp. 3–4.

p. 43 *he was scary*: Dennis Mohr and Hava Gurevich, *Disfarmer: A Portrait of America* (Toronto: Public Pictures, 2014).

p. 43 *as a 'weirdo'*: Mohr and Gurevich.

p. 43 *on the street*: Mohr and Gurevich.

p. 46 *often ignored and overlooked*: Laura Wilson, 'Background', in Richard Avedon, *In the American West, 1979–1984* (New York: Harry N. Abrams, Inc., 1985). Cited in 'In the American East: Richard Avedon Incorporated', Richard Bolton (ed.), *The Contest of Meaning: Critical Histories of Photography* (Cambridge: MIT, 1992), p. 263.

p. 47 *speaking through his eyes*: Wilson, p. 267.

p. 48 *so powerful and so immediate*: Mohr and Gurevich.

p. 49 local community of picture finders: Mohr and Gurevich.

p. 49 *radius of Disfarmer's studio*: Mohr and Gurevich.

p. 50 *level or condition report*s: Eren Orbey 'Who Owns Mike Disfarmer's Photographs?', *The New Yorker*, 13 July 2021, p. 25.

p. 50 *a feeding frenzy*: Orbey, p. 26.

p. 50 *my grandmother to money*: Mohr and Gurevich.

p. 50 *for between $7,500 – $24,000 each*: Orbey, p. 26.

p. 51 *transferring wealth*: Orbey, p. 25.

p. 52 *Charles was scared*: Mohr and Gurevich.

p. 53 *whatever that theatre was*: Mohr and Gurevich.

p. 54 *capture what they're all about*: Mohr and Gurevich.

p. 55 *Zorro-like figure*: Michael Mattis 'Rediscovering Disfarmer', from *Disfarmer, The Vintage Prints* (New York: Powerhouse Books, 2005).

p. 56 *a rebel who stayed at home*: Jenny Maria Nilsson, 'The Photographer in their Midst' in Janne Jönsson, *John Alinder. Portraits 1910–32* (Stockport: Dewi Lewis Publishing, 2021), p. 252.

p. 60 *where no one wanted to live*: André Magnin (ed.), *Seydou Keïta* (Zurich: Scalo, 1997), p. 9.

p. 60 *Art is beauty*: Magnin, pp. 11–12.

p. 62 *she also liked it*: Magnin, p. 11.

p. 63 *but it was all haphazard*: Magnin, p. 12.

p. 64 *keep the negative*: Okwui Enwezor, 'Samuel Fosso and the Invention of the Artist as a Young Photographer', in *Aperture*, 13 August 2020.

p. 65 *with African photography*: Enwezor.

p. 67 *studio portraiture*: Silvia Rosi interviewed by Eric Otieno Sumba, *GRIOT*, 08/07/2020.

p. 74 *Paignton studio*: some photographs by J. Rawlings of Paignton are in the National Trust's collection at Laycock Abbey.

Photography's Realism

p. 80 *assertive naturalism*: Martin Kemp, *The Science of Art: Optical Themes in Western Art from Brunelleschi to Seurat* (New Haven: Yale University Press, 1990), p. 132.

p. 81 *to reflect light*: Clovis Whitfield, *Caravaggio's Eye* (London, Paul Holberton, 2011), p. 230.

p. 82 *camera obscura*: Philip Steadman, *Vermeer's Camera* (Oxford: Oxford University Press, 2002).

p. 82 *(1660–1663)*: Martin Bailey, *Vermeer* (London: Phaidon, 1995), pp. 60–62.

p. 83 *as luminous globules*: Kemp, pp. 193–194.

p. 85 *map-work*: Henry Fuseli, 1831, vol. 2, p. 217. Cited in John Bonehill and Stephen Daniels (ed.), *Paul Sandby. Picturing Britain* (London: Royal Academy of Arts, 2009).

p. 85 *of a given spot*: Henry Fuseli, cited in Michael Rosenthal and Anne Lyles, *Turner and Constable: Sketching from Nature* (London: Tate Publishing, 2013), p. 27.

p. 89 *are but the experiments*: John Constable, quoted in C.R. Leslie, *Memoirs of the Life of John Constable*, 2nd ed. (London: 1845), p. 355.

p. 89 *les devants*: Pierre-Henri de Valenciennes, *Réflexions et conseils à un élève sur la peinture* (Paris, 1820), cited in Ger Luijten 'Skies and Effects', p. 154; in Ger Luijten, Mary Morton and Jane Munro, *True to Nature. Open-air Painting in Europe 1780–1870* (London: Paul Holberton Publishing, 2020).

p. 89 *going skoying*: Gilpin 1792, p. 34, in 'Notes to "On Landscape Painting, A Poem"'; see Hawes 1969, pp. 348–49.

p. 92 *the accurate delineation*: Edward Dodwell, *Classical and Topographical Tour through Greece during the Years 1801, 1805, and 1806. I*, pp. 565–69. Cited in John McKesson Camp II, *In Search of Greece* (Los Altos: The Packard Humanities Institute, 2013), p. 84.

p. 93 *historic tide levels*: Hugh Aldersey-Williams, *Tide* (London: Viking, 2016), p. 120.

p. 94 *Towne's probate*: Richard Stephens in correspondence with the author.

p. 95 *sun-pictures themselves*: William Henry Fox Talbot, *Sun pictures in Scotland* (London, 1845).

p. 96 *would subsequently reveal*: Larry Schaaf, *Out of the Shadows: Herschel, Talbot, and the Invention of*

Photography (New Haven: Yale University Press, 1992), p. 158.

p. 96 *could only occasionally visit*: cited in Mike Chrimes, *Civil Engineering 1839–1889: a Photographic History* (Stroud: Budding Books, 1997), p. 12.

p. 97 *that-has-been*: Roland Barthes, *Camera Lucid*a (Vintage, London, 2000), p. 96.

p. 99 *the plaster cast*: Oliver Wendell Holmes classified photographs as 'morphotypes' or 'form-prints', distinguishing them from 'logo-types' or words. Cited in Stephen C. Pinson, *Monumental Journey: the Daguerrotypes of Girault de Prangey* (New York: The Metropolitan Museum of Art, 2019) p. 25.

p. 99 *Classical ideal*: J. J. Winckelmann, *Geschichte der Kunst des Alterthums* (Dresden, 1764), pp. 147–48; 2nd ed Vienna, 1776, p. 257 (reprint edited by A. H. Borbein et al., Johann Joachim Winckelmann, *Geschichte der Kunst des Alterthums,* Johann Joachim Winckelmann, *Schriften und Nachlass*, vol IV, 1 (Mainz, 2002), p. 249). Cited in Marc Felmann, 'Under the Light of Helios: early photography and the Parthenon sculptures', *Sculpture Journal*, 15.2 (2006), p. 164.

p. 99 *the genuine article*: É.-M. Falconet, *Œuvres*, vol. 1 (Lausanne 1781), pp. 271 and 314–15. Cited in Marc Felmann, 'Under the light of Helios: early photography and the Parthenon sculptures', *Sculpture Journal*, 15.2 2006, pp. 164–5.

p. 99 *Elgin Marbles*: Felmann, p. 167.

p. 99 *archaeography*: Michael Shanks and Connie Svabo, 'Photography and Archaeology: a Pragmatology', in *Reclaiming Archaeology Beyond the Tropes of Modernity*, ed. Alfredo González-Ruibal (New York: Routledge, 2013), pp. 89–103. Cited in Pinson, p. 10.

p. 99 *short space of time*: François Agaro, 1839, p. 235.

p. 100 *camera obscura*: Olivier Caumont, 'From Drawing to Photography: Image Production Techniques', in Stephen C. Pinson, p. 176. Olivier Caumont hypothesises that Girault de Prangey favoured the *camera lucida*.

p. 101 *pure philology*: Joseph-Philibert Girault de Prangey, letter to Thomas Leverton Donaldson, 30 March 1847. Cited in Stephen C. Pinson, p. 25.

p. 101 *rectangular boxes*: Joseph Charles de Simony, *Un curieuse figure d'artiste: Girault de Prangey, 1804–1892* (Dijon: J. Belvet, 1937), p. 10. Cited in 'The Odyssey of an Artist and his Work', Sylvie Aubenas, p. 5, in Pinson.

p. 103 *his verbal attacks*: Joseph Charles de Simony.

p. 104 *Cheyenne, Wyoming*: Toby Jurovics, *Framing the West: the Survey Photographs of Timothy H. O'Sullivan* (Washington: Library of Congress, 2010), p. 9.

p. 106 *astonishing realism*: 'That the photograph of the 1850s did not produce color or clouds or anything moving, that the world it depicted was largely vacant, was very quickly taken for granted and such deficiencies discussed almost exclusively in the context of the critical debate that focused on photography versus painting.' Abigail Solomon-Godeau, 'A Photographer in Jerusalem', *October*, Autumn 1981, Vol. 18, p. 98.

p. 106 *their validity as art*: Rosalind Krauss, 'Photography's Discursive Spaces', *Art Journal*, vol. 42, no. 4, 1982. Reproduced in Richard Bolton, *The Contest of Meaning. Critical Histories of Photography* (Cambridge: MIT Press, 1989) p. 287.

p. 106 *by O'Sullivan*: Krauss, p. 288.

p. 107 *exhibitionality*: Krauss, p. 288.

p. 107 *who took the picture*: Krauss, p. 291.

p. 107 *as he worked*: Jurovics, p. 19.

p. 111 *just one year?*: Krauss, p. 293.

p. 111 *steely-eyed daguerreotype*: although the French photographer Gustave Le Gray (1820–1884) modified the calotype process by waxing the sheet of silver iodide, which gave the image a more pronounced definition.

p. 112 *une brutalité concluante*: Auguste Salzmann, *Jerusalem* (Paris, 1856), p. 4. Cited in Frederick N. Bohrer, *Photography and Architecture* (London: Reaktion, 2011), p. 105. Bohrer (and Abigail Solomon-Godeau) translates this phrase as 'a conclusive brute force'; the translation I prefer is by Roger Leverdier.

p. 113 *gazette of local industry*: in conversation with the author, Düsseldorf, 2002.

p. 114 *on the observer*: Hilla Becher in conversation with James Lingwood, *The Music of the Blast Furnaces* in *Art Press* 209, January 1996, pp. 21–28. Cited in Susanne Lange, *Bernd and Hilla Becher. Life and Work* (Cambridge, Mass.: MIT Press, 2007), p. 195.

p. 115 *way to do that*: Lange, p. 192.

p. 115 *this industrial age*: Lange, p. 192.

p. 115 *not the enemy, of art*: Peter Galassi, Wall text for NY MoMA exhibition of *Bernd and Hilla Becher*, 2008.

p. 117 *if they are comparable*: Bernd Becher in conversation with James Lingwood, *The Music of the Blast Furnaces* in *Art Press* 209, January 1996, pp. 21–28.

p. 117 *Minimalist and Conceptual Art*: for example, *Konzeption-conception: Dokumentation einer heutigen Kunstrichtung* (Leverkusen Schloss Morsbroich: Stadtisches Museum, 1969).

p. 118 *a bigger version*: Thomas Ruff in conversation at The Whitechapel Gallery, London. 2017.

p. 119 *considered too low*: when Rover Cars closed their Longbridge factory, they threw their photography archive into skips. I was able to salvage some and deliver it to Birmingham Central Library. The entire black and white photography archive of English China Clays in Cornwall has disappeared. Archives in Britain remain unprotected by legislation.

p. 120 *fragments the art*: Abigail Solomon-Godeau, 'A Photographer in Jerusalem, 1855: Auguste Salzmann and His Times', *October*, Autumn 1981, Vol. 18, p. 107.

The Family Silver

p. 128 *drawing its outline*: Pliny the Elder, *Natural History*, Book 35 v 15 and xliii 151, cited in Andreas Beyer, *Portraits, A History* (Abrams: New York, 2003), p. 17.

p. 129 *called Jimmy Forsyth*: Jimmy Forsyth, *Scotswood Road*, ed. Derek Smith (Newcastle upon Tyne: Bloodaxe Books, 1986).

p. 130 *of human existence*: Richard Brilliant, *Portraiture* (London: Reaktion Books, 1991), p. 14.

p. 131 *that-has-been*: Roland Barthes, *Camera Lucida* (London: Vintage, 2000), p. 96.

p. 131 *disclose or reveal*: Andreas Beyer, p. 16.

p. 132 *colour slide film*: other types of slide (or 'positive') film include Agfachrome, Fujichrome and Ilfachrome.

p. 136 *unassuming nature*: Conal Shields in conversation with the author, London, 2018.

p. 137 *the colours are warmer*: excluded are slides where the colours have shifted very significantly due to poor archival qualities.

Blind Corners

p. 164 *Death of the Author*: 'Classic criticism has never paid any attention to the reader; for it, the writer is the only person in literature [...] we know that to give writing its future, it is necessary to overthrow the myth: the birth of the reader must be at the cost of the death of the Author.' Roland Barthes, *The Death of the Author* (1967).

p. 166 *through psychoanalysis*: Walter Benjamin, 'A Short History of Photography', *Literarische Welt* (Sept, Oct, 1931).

p. 166 *Mickey Mouse*: Walter Benjamin 'The Work of Art in Its Age of Technological Reproducibility', second version (1936) in Walter Benjamin: *Selected Writings, Vol.3, 1931–1938*, trans. Rodney Livingstone et al., ed. Michael W. Jennings, Howard Eiland, and Gary Smith (Cambridge, Mass: Belknap, 2020), p. 117.

p. 167 *dream-world*: Susan Buck-Morss, 'The Flaneur, the Sandwichman and the Whore: the Politics of Loitering', *New German Critique* 39 (Autumn 1986), p. 109. Cited in Shawn Michelle Smith and Sharon Sliwinski, ed., *Photography and the Optical Unconscious* (Durham and London: Duke University Press, 2017), p. 10.

p. 180 *unprinted negative*: Sigmund Freud, *Moses and Monotheism* (1939), in SE, vol. 23, pp. 125–126. Cited in Smith and Sliwinski, p. 13.

p. 167 *the uncanny*: Sigmund Freud, 'The Uncanny', *The Standard Edition of the Complete Psychological Works of Sigmund Freud*, Vol. 17 (London: The Hogarth Press, 1925), pp. 219–253.

p. 167 *secretly familiar*: Freud, p. 241.

ACKNOWLEDGEMENTS

I am very grateful to my editor Rosalind Porter for her belief in publishing this book, to Louise Tucker for her diligent copyediting, and to Will Self for his percipient introduction.

Roger Leverdier and Audrey Reeder read and reread my drafts, providing advice and insights without which these essays would be lesser versions. I cannot thank you sufficiently.

I would also like to thank Ryan Harding, who rescued the Blind Corner negatives and applied his digital expertise to numerous other reproductions.

Thomas Struth kindly gave me permission to reproduce his *Crosby Street, Soho, New York*, 1978.

I wish I were able to thank those uncredited photographers who remain anonymous. You're in the firmament. As is Salome, the Western lowland gorilla. My thanks, too, to Graham Hughes, for his kindness and trust, and to Dick Jewell, Sandor Kardos, Camilla Lööf at Uplandsmuseet and Anne-Guylaine Forêt at the Musée de Langres.

So many other people helped me along the way, and I am very grateful to you all, in particular, Liz Jobey, Andrew Gardiner, Joey Sharp and Marie-Laure Davenport.

All of the above are utterly blameless for any of the views expressed in any of the essays.

PHOTO CREDITS

Coronation Day, Tenby, 1953 © Graham Hughes; *Linda DaVolls and Salome*, 1992 © Michael Collins; John Alinder, c.1910–20 © Upplandsmuseet; *Seydou Keïta, untitled and undated* © The Jean Pigozzi African Art Collection; *Russian soldiers*, c.1946, Photographer unknown © Sandor Kardos; Photobooth photograph, date unknown © Dick Jewell; Francis Towne, *No. 21 Inside the Colosea*, 1780 © The Trustees of the British Museum; Joseph-Philibert Girault de Prangey, *Porte Gallo-Romaine, Langres*, c.1847 © Musée de Langres; Timothy H. O'Sullivan, *The Pyramid & Domes, Pyramid Lake, Nevada*, 1867 © Library of Congress; *Crosby Street, Soho, New York*, 1978 © Thomas Struth; Jimmy Forsyth, *Outside the Royal Oak, Scotswood Road*, 1956 © Tyne and Wear Archives; *Hoo St Werburgh*, 2014 © Michael Collins; *Hoo Flats*, 2016 © Michael Collins; *Blind Corners* © Michael Collins.

Other titles from Notting Hill Editions*

The Catastrophe Hour: Selected Essays
Meghan Daum

'For the last five or six years, on many afternoons around 4 or
5 p.m., I've been overcome with the sensation that my life is
effectively over. This is not a sensation of the world ending; it's
a distinct feeling of being at the end of my days. My time, while
technically not "up," is disappearing in the rearview mirror.
The fact that this feeling of ambient doom tends to coincide
with the blue-tinged, pre-gloaming light of the late afternoon
lends to the whole thing a cosmic beauty, as devastating as it is
awe-inspiring. As such, I've dubbed this the catastrophe hour.'

Written between 2016 and 2024, these essays are classic Daum,
showcasing her wit, her intellect and her uncanny ability to
throw new light on even the most ubiquitous of subjects.
Delving into divorce, dating, music, friendship, beauty, aging,
death and money, Daum's unflinching honesty and exacting
observations secure her reputation as one of our most important
and enduring essayists.

Outrage
Ian Nairn
Introduced by Travis Elborough

In 1955, Britain's most prestigious architectural magazine,
The Architectural Review, published a special issue featuring
a single essay by Ian Nairn, a famously opinionated (and
untrained) architectural critic. Based on observations made
on a journey Nairn took across the UK in a Morris Minor,
Outrage is a searing critique of urban sprawl, or 'Subtopia'. In
this manifesto, Nairn warns that 'if what is called development
is allowed to multiply at the present rate', Britain's natural –
and urban – landscapes will lose their individuality and spirit.
A call-to-arms against the 'greying out' of our towns and
countryside before it's too late, *Outrage* is widely considered to
be Nairn's masterpiece.

The Penalty Kick: The Story of a Gamechanger
Robert McCrum

'Football in the 1880s was an unruly, rough, and often dangerous game. To curb the state the sport was in, William McCrum proposed a new and drastic sanction. He called it a penalty kick.'

In 1891, a contentious new measure against an excess of foul play, Rule 13, was proposed to the FA by an amateur goalkeeper from County Armagh. 'The Irishman's Motion' modernised the world's most popular game. Today – in the shootout – Rule 13 continues to influence the sport through its astonishing psychological grip on our imaginations. A tale of sportsmanship, chance and obsession, *The Penalty Kick* explores both the addiction of risk, and a doomed father-son relationship that could have been torn from the pages of a late-Victorian novel, inspired by the edgy, ruthless and egalitarian spirit of Northern Ireland.

Things I Don't Want to Know
Deborah Levy

'Perhaps when Orwell described sheer egoism as a necessary quality for a writer, he was not thinking about the sheer egoism of a female writer. Even the most arrogant female writer has to work over time to build an ego that is robust enough to get her through January, never mind all the way to December.'

Taking Orwell's famous list of motives for writing as the jumping-off point for a sequence of thrilling reflections on the writing life, *Things I Don't Want to Know* is a is a perfect companion not just to Orwell's essay, but also to Levy's own, essential oeuvre.

What We Talk About When We Talk About Crime
Jennifer Fleetwood

Over the past few decades, there has been a remarkable rise in the number of people who speak publicly about their experience of crime. These personal accounts used to be confined to the police station and the courtroom, but today bookshops heave with autobiographies by prisoners, criminals, police and barristers while streaming platforms host hours of interviews with serial killers, death-row residents, vigilantes and gang members. In *What We Talk About When We Talk About Crime*, criminologist Jennifer Fleetwood examines seven infamous crime stories to make sense of this modern confessional impulse, including Howard Marks's outlandish autobiography *Mr Nice*, Shamima Begum's controversial *Times* interview, Prince Andrew's disastrous *Newsnight* appearance and Myra Hindley's unpublished prison letters.

Lewis Carroll's Guide for Insomniacs
Introduced by Gyles Brandreth

'The dilemma my friends suppose me to be in,' writes the author of *Alice's Adventures in Wonderland*, 'has, for its two horns, the endurance of a sleepless night, and the adoption of some recipe for inducing sleep.' In this delightful book – the perfect gift for all insomniacs – are collected a splendid variety of entertainments devised to help pass 'the wakeful hours'.

Ranging from puzzles, rhymes and limericks to simple number problems, calming calculations and planning dreams, *Lewis Carroll's Guide for Insomniacs* is a feast of intriguing activities guaranteed to keep you entertained as you search for the elusive rabbit-hole of a good night's sleep.

How Shostakovich Changed my Mind
Stephen Johnson

Winner of the 2021 Rubery Book Award

In this powerfully honest and brilliant book, BBC music broadcaster Stephen Johnson explores the impact of Shostakovich's music during Stalin's reign of terror and writes – at the same time – of the extraordinary healing effect of music on the mind. As someone who has lived with bipolar disorder for most of his life, Johnson looks at neurological, psychotherapeutic and philosophical findings, and reflects on his own experience of how Shostakovich's music helped him survive the trials and assaults of mental illness.

I Remember
Joe Brainard, Introduced by Paul Auster

Joe Brainard's *I Remember* is a cult classic, envied and admired by writers from Frank O'Hara to John Ashbery and Edmund White. As autobiography, Brainard's method was brilliantly simple: to set down specific memories ('everything is interesting, sooner or later') as they rose to the surface of his consciousness, each prefaced by the refrain 'I remember'.

Cary Grant's Suit:
Nine Movies That Made Me the Wreck I Am Today
Todd McEwen

Todd McEwen grew up in Southern California. As the son of relatively normal people, he had no in with Hollywood, a mere thirteen miles away, try as he might. This is a kid who loved the movies so much, he got up at 4.30 in the morning to watch Laurel and Hardy. A kid who made his father project 8mm cartoons onto the family's dining room curtains so they could be slowly parted, just like at a real cinema. A guy who based his philosophy of life on Captain Nemo, and has watched *Chinatown* over sixty times. So far.

A Strange Life: Selected Essays of Louisa May Alcott
Edited by Liz Rosenberg and introduced by Jane Smiley

Louisa May Alcott is best known as the author of *Little Women*.
But she was also a noted essayist who wrote on a wide range of
subjects, including her father's failed utopian commune, life as
a Civil War nurse and her experience as a young woman sent to
work in service to alleviate her family's poverty. Blending gentle
satire with reportage and emotive biography, *A Strange Life*
– edited by Liz Rosenberg and with a preface by Jane Smiley
– shows Alcott to be one of the sharpest wits in American
literature.

A Garden from a Hundred Packets of Seed
James Fenton

'It seemed a simple and interesting idea: what plants would you
choose if starting a garden from scratch, given that you were
only allowed to propagate them from seed? The emphasis is on
childish simplicity of approach, and economy of outlay.'

In *A Garden From a Hundred Packets of Seed* – a light-hearted
gardening book – James Fenton describes a hundred plants he
would choose to grow from seed. Flowers for colour, size, or
exotic interest; herbs and meadow flowers; climbing vines and
tropical species . . . Here is a happy, stylish, thought-provoking
exercise in good principles, which exudes that rare thing:
common-or-garden sense about gardens.

*All titles are available in the UK, and some titles are available
in the rest of the world. For more information please visit
www.nottinghilleditions.com.

A selection of our titles is distributed in the US and Canada by
New York Review Books. For more information on available
titles please visit www.nyrb.com